T0148969

PRAISE FOR THE IMPACT BOOK

"Simon himself has impact. He used a winning combination of insights, practical tools and humour to help me and many of the teams I have led to significantly enhance our impact and function more effectively as a team."
Brenda Trenownden, Managing Director,
Head of FIG Europe, ANZ Bank

"We're proud to work with Simon as one of our Coachmatch partner coaches and a member of a number of our client panels – he brings great expertise supporting senior leaders to build their impact, presence and leadership brand."
Trudi Ryan, CEO, Coachmatch

"I needed to change my impact as I took on a new role – Simon not only helped me do that but made me more effective as a business person. I'm more rounded, more reasoned and ultimately, more effective. His approach and his tools can make a difference very quickly."
Gordon Roberston, Director of Communications,
Edinburgh Airport and Chair of Marketing Edinburgh

"Simon has incredible intuitive insight. He uses this skill to get the people he works with to focus on the important issues. He disarms their inhibitions and turns impact into focused, deliberate and intentionful impact."

Warren L Creates, Head of Immigration Law Group, Perley-Robertson, Hill & McDougall LLP

"From day one working with Simon he shifted me from doubt to belief about being a world leading sprint coach and the impact I could have in athletics. I now stand as one of the leaders nationally in my field and truly believe being the world's best simply awaits me on my path, I owe a huge chunk of my success to his guidance."

Dan Cossins, former Great Britain Junior Sprints and Relays Coach

THE IMPACT BOOK

50 WAYS TO ENHANCE YOUR PRESENCE AND IMPACT AT WORK

SIMON TYLER

LONDON
MADRID
MEXICO CITY
NEW YORK
BARCELONA
MONTERREY
SHANGHAI
BOGOTA
BUENOS AIRES
SAN FRANCISCO

Published by
LID Publishing Limited
The Record Hall, Studio 204,
16-16a Baldwins Gardens,
London EC1N 7RJ, UK

524 Broadway, 11th Floor, Suite 08-120,
New York, NY 10012, US

info@lidpublishing.com
www.lidpublishing.com

www.businesspublishersroundtable.com

First edition published in 2015 under the title *The Impact Code*

Printed in Latvia by Jelgavas Tipogrāfij

ISBN: 978-1-911498-69-8

Cover and page design: Caroline Li and Matthew Renaudin

FOR OTHER TITLES IN THE SERIES...

CLEVER CONTENT, DYNAMIC IDEAS, PRACTICAL SOLUTIONS AND ENGAGING VISUALS – A CATALYST TO INSPIRE NEW WAYS OF THINKING AND PROBLEM-SOLVING IN A COMPLEX WORLD

conciseadvicelab.com

TO THE READER,
MAY YOU HAVE THE IMPACT
YOU TRULY DESIRE

CONTENTS

ACKNOWLEDGEMENTS

This book would not exist without the efforts, nurturing, nudging and kindness of many people, specifically Dr Fran Wilby, Rachelle Mills and Simon Emmett who have worked with me, keeping me true to task and on schedule.

My close friends and family have all been immense supporters, listening ears and reliable friends, particularly over some challenging recent years, thank you.

My sincere thanks extends to many others:

To Martin Liu and the team at LID who provided their editorial assistance, insight and ideas.

To my clients with whom I have worked up many of the Impact Notes you will read here.

To my children, my family and many friends who have and continue to enrich my life in more ways than I can express. If my impact is measured by those in my circles, I am delighted with it all!

Thank you all.

FOREWORD

The fact that you are holding and reading this book suggests to me that you are at least curious about impact. Your impact.

Perhaps you sense you could have greater impact but aren't quite managing it yet. Perhaps your results are a mish-mash of what you want and nothing like what you want. In any case there will be an Impact Note in here that will stir your thinking, inspire you to take more deliberate action or even to reconsider what you are actually up to and involved in today!

If you and I were working together in person we would explore where you are right now and what is showing up for you as a result of the impact you are causing. In our conversations we would undoubtedly explore what many of the Impact Notes discuss, and use them to inspire impactful change in you. Without the conversation I obviously don't know where to point you first, so begin at the beginning and allow your intuition to enjoy the chapters, take to heart those that resonate (you will feel it, and know it) and let go those notes that don't (you'll feel or know that too. It will be distinct).

While *The Impact Book* cannot compare to a coaching or mentoring dialogue, work with each chapter as if it had come from such a conversation and experiment with the suggested thinking and actions.

My one-on-one and one-on-team coaching work has allowed me to experience many of the challenges of impact and to explore and experiment with my clients on what brings positive change. This book houses 50 of those pearls of wisdom.

Simon Tyler
December 2017

INTRODUCTION

Every one of us has impact. You have impact. All the time.

Success, personally and professionally, is in direct correlation with the impact you intend.

Your impact equates to...
Purposeful intent x clarity and consistency
... in everything that you are and everything that you do.

For the purposes of this book, the term 'impact' is used to describe the effect you have on events and on those around you. Having impact expresses the collective impression left by your visual appearance; your presence; the way you connect with others; what you say; how you behave and the lasting effect you have on people after you leave the room.

The Impact Book will help you notice how some people can have such a deep impact on others and to harness this for yourself.

IMPACT WITHOUT MINDFULNESS IS FLAWED

Without mindfulness, without purpose and authentic intention, irrespective of your dramatic style upgrades, your impact is left impotent and empty. True leaders and innovators – Gandhi, Martin Luther-King, Winston Churchill, Steve Jobs – are considered 'great' based on their passion, and their belief in their purpose:

People wanted to follow and believe in their ideas.

Without a sense of what motivates and inspires you, a new suit or different haircut will do little to improve your leadership potential.

THE IMPACT OF FIRST IMPRESSIONS

First impressions are formed quickly, often unconsciously, and they matter. Researchers from New York University found people make 11 major decisions about one another in the first seven seconds of meeting. These judgements are based on a mixture of conscious and unconscious reactions to appearance, gestures, stance, tone of voice, conversational openers, and they establish the foundations for our ongoing relationships.

Through heightening your awareness, evaluating, then adapting the impact you have on others, you can ensure the best possible impact more often and in all your modes of communication. It matters because you cannot possibly predict how interactions can blossom; from a chance meeting comes a key client; from a brief conversation comes a job offer. Impact isn't only about the 'big' moments in your professional life, it is about being present in every moment; this shift in thinking signals your intention that every encounter has the potential to bring something to you, financially, professionally, or personally.

THE IMPACT OF FIRST IMPRESSIONS

The scale of your impact can be measured in terms of how clearly what you intend is coming to pass. That scale could be measured by the volume of your friends, colleagues, and associates that know, with clarity, what it is you intend and in some way are involved in that coming to pass too.

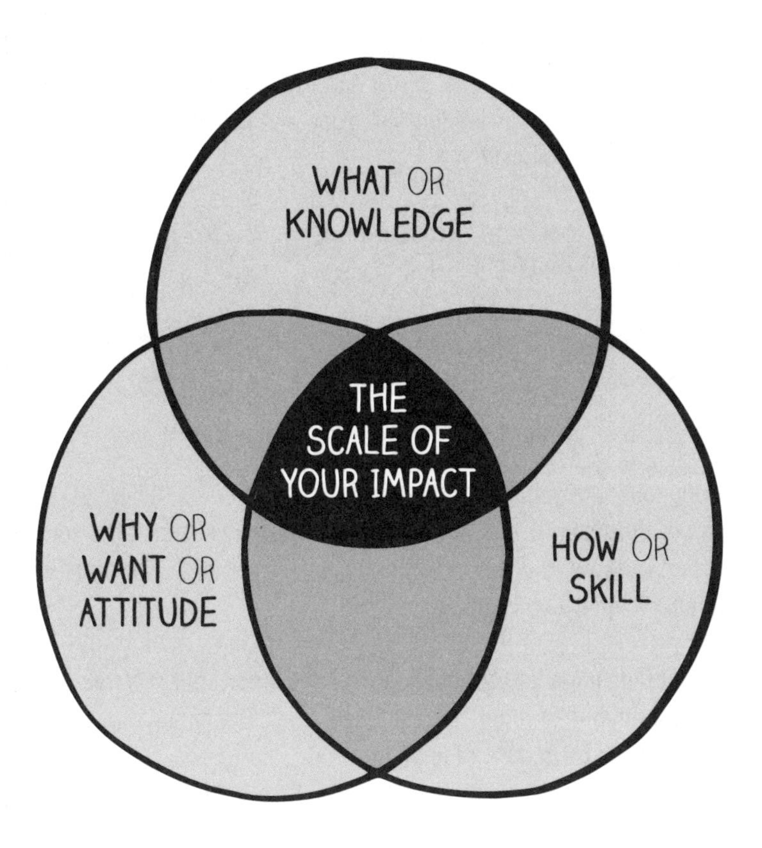

You may have seen this diagram many times before, its simplicity serves us well here again.

Your impact is the overlap of the three sections. The size of each circle reflects your success in that topic and the consistency with which it is your way, every day.

1. Why or Want or Attitude – this has been termed 'your truth'. What sits underneath? What is you purpose? What are your unique skills, experiences leading you to be and do? Why bother even having any impact?

2. What or Knowledge – What is it that you intend? How clear are you on that intention? How might you know?

3. How or Skill – all the aspects of how you show up, who you are, how you communicate, awareness of the ways and methods and effectiveness of causing impact.

Notionally rate yourself in the three areas out of 10. Where 10 is clarity, consistency and certainty, and 1 would be uncertain, confused, variable. And simply where the circles are large, the scale of impact intersection is greater.

Each of the Impact Notes or chapters will support your performance upgrade in one or more of these three areas. The cumulative effect of which will be enhanced impact!

HOW TO USE THIS BOOK

The chapters in *The Impact Book* are named Impact Notes and each relates to a challenge to your thinking, to your current habits and behaviours and suggests specific actions you can take now, today, to shift the way in which you see yourself, and the way in which others perceive you. You could:

- Read the Impact Notes in order
  - ◇ Mark those that instantly resonate and take action
  - ◇ Take action on one note every week

- Randomly open *The Impact Book* and work with the note in front of you.

- Scan the list of contents and take in those that feel most relevant to you, today, and begin there.

I'm determined that this book will shift from just being a good read to inspiring you to take action.

Try to change something in your routine, week by week. Introduce one idea at a time in order to absorb fully the shift in thought and practice. If you can use just some of the thinking and ideas contained in the Impact Code of Practice, you will experience real change;

if you work with all 50 Impact Notes, your life path will transform and you will be taking deliberate steps to becoming a purposeful, powerful leader.

YOUR 'A' GAME

As with the pursuit of 'A' grades at school, your 'A' game is, quite simply, you at your best. In leadership, this is about creating truly inspiring connections with your team, your peers, and your clients and stakeholders. Powerful, authentic leadership can be identified by four escalating outcomes:

a) Attraction
b) Appetite
c) Advocacy
d) Action

Attraction – People are attracted to you and to your ideas. They may, or may not, be able to explain why, but they gravitate towards you in a room and are eager to hear what you have to say.

Appetite – Your connection with individuals amplifies their initial attraction; they are now actively aware of their interest in your ideas, your team, your company, and they want more.

Advocacy – People are deeply and passionately aware of your ideas and motivated to advocate them to others – they support your cause verbally, they discuss it with peers, creating a buzz around you and your vision.

Action – Your passion and leadership create a palpable and obvious response in others. They take new, inspired action, and do something directly as a result of their involvement with you. You create change through the actions of others. Your impact is spreading more widely and is not restricted to the people you meet in person.

These four Leadership Impact outcomes describe how your energy, behaviour and ideas can ripple outwards, creating an excitement and passion in others (or not!). The initial attraction is created by your own belief in what you do and your ability to communicate to others *why* it is important. What is it about your business that motivates you, your staff and your customers? When you identify this core, the fire of your passion ignites and draws others to you. Their appetite grows, encouraging further engagement, and their support and advocacy gradually strengthens, driving them to positive action; this is pure and simple leadership.

Many leaders I have observed emit very different visual, verbal and physical messages than those they intend. Do yours? Heightening your self-awareness, becoming more deliberate, will enhance your impact and accelerate the pace of the change you desire, and with it many of the spoils you seek, material, emotional and spiritual.

The Impact Book provides a roadmap to building (or perhaps rebuilding) positive and impactful perceptions of you and your work.

ATTRACTION:

FINDING YOUR LEADERSHIP MAGNETISM

"THE GREATER DANGER FOR MOST OF US LIES NOT IN SETTING OUR AIM TOO HIGH AND FALLING SHORT; BUT IN SETTING OUR AIM TOO LOW, AND ACHIEVING OUR MARK."

Michelangelo

THE FOLLOWING CHAPTERS CHALLENGE YOU TO CONSIDER WHY PEOPLE SHOULD FOLLOW YOU. WHAT ATTRACTS THEM? THESE IMPACT NOTES INVITE YOU TO EXPLORE YOUR PURPOSE AND YOUR AIMS IN AN AUTHENTIC WAY.

1. PURPOSE

Where better to begin your impact journey than with purpose? The question "what is your purpose?" is timeless, most people have paused to contemplate this and just as many have given up, disillusioned by their inability to articulate their reason for being, to justify their existence on earth.

This first Impact Note is a foundation stone for your Impact Code, and seeks to unravel tangled thoughts and ways of going about this hunt for purpose.

Let's be clear, purpose is not permanent; purpose is almost never one thing.

Read that again. Simply recognizing this impermanence can be liberating. If, by any chance, you have times in your life during which you feel you have purpose, treat this purpose lightly, don't cling to it too tightly. Let it go when needs be and be open to embracing a greater purpose that, almost certainly, is about to emerge.

The act of finding purpose is, by its nature, elusive. Purpose evolves and emerges and only, to a tiny extent, in response to searching for it; 'allowing' is the more relevant action here.

And another thing; your purpose has nothing to do with what you do. Your purpose is about discovering and nurturing who you truly are, knowing yourself at the deepest level and guiding yourself back when you lose your way.

Any and all of the impact you have in the world will correlate to your (constantly emerging and evolving) purpose.

In absolute and simple terms there are only three things to do:

a) Decide to be open to recognizing your purpose
b) Identify, expand and express your talents
c) Find more ways and places in which you can use your talents

To support your journey here is a simple Six Step Purpose Toolkit I have shaped over my years of coaching and mentoring, and drawn from the lessons I have learned from inspirational masters (see the Further Reading section on page 161) from across the globe:

SOMEONE ELSE'S PURPOSE

Are you on a path signposted to you by your parents, your peers, the media, society? Does it really make you happy? Evaluate what you want/where are you heading, and run it past the following triage a few times (each go can uncover a deeper level of thinking):

- Why do I want that?
- What then?
- What will I have or be then?

AWAY FROM OR TOWARDS

You will be surrounded by a rich mix of 'push and pull' forces, none of which are inherently good or bad, they are simply forces. Identify those that you can. What are the situations, roles, people, events, places, circumstances to which you are drawn? What are the situations, roles, people, events, places, circumstances from which you are moving away or by which you are repulsed?

TURNAROUND

What are the contingent changes for which you are waiting or which need to be in place before what you really want can become possible? For example, complete a few sentences using "when or if ... (this is true)..., I'll then ..." The turnaround works by flipping that sentence around and noticing your thoughts and feelings then. Through exploring the contingency you can uncover your desires and passions; there they sit, masked by the annoying excuse or obstacle.

NATURALLY

What are the things you do naturally, almost mindlessly, and possibly take for granted? Your colleagues and friends may often say "it comes naturally to you". Do you have an eye for detail, a sense of humour, a way of engaging newcomers, an ability to think way ahead? This is your talent, this is where your genius shows up. Look for clues.

LOVE IT

This is so obvious it should be where you start, but its simplicity often makes it the least actioned part of your purpose work. Simply list as many things as you can that you love (I use this word deliberately to stir you to go beyond the 'like' and 'quite enjoy' items). The activities, places, people that make you smile, that have an impact on you. You deeply enjoy being involved in or with these people or things. If you enjoyed complete financial freedom you would still be absorbed by them. Your leadership life is not about waiting for these things, or squeezing them into the gaps in your itinerary. They form the fabric of your life and almost certainly will inform the nature of your authentic and purposeful impact.

THE INSPIRERS

Throughout your life you will have noticed and emulated certain people, consciously or unconsciously, and their inspiration for you lives on. List the six to 10 people who you admire the most, by whom you are most inspired and motivated. Next to each name write down one word or phrase that captures the inspirational nugget they represent for you. For example, Mother Teresa – selflessness, Winston Churchill – wisdom and statesmanship, Usain Bolt – absolute self-belief. Re-write the nuggets on a separate page, these are now yours, describing the leadership impact you are destined to have, to be used to inform the choices and decisions on your journey towards this.

Now turn these freshly written-down thoughts into action. Read your work every day for 10 days, each time pausing to consider how your words make you feel. The physical and emotional response will provide clues to the places from which your purpose will emerge.

2. AUTHENTIC YOU

Authentic leadership is discussed and written about so often that it has gained the accolade of being termed 'an approach' to leadership rather than just a description. It has become a study for leadership academics.

Authentic means 'from the source'. Retail products and brands often extol the virtues of their product being original (from the origin) and pure.

Authentic leadership, then, is about you operating from your source, that guiding light deep within you; being the best version of you, behaving and acting in the manner that comes instinctively to you.

In Ancient Greek philosophy, authenticity simply meant being in control of your own life. This is centred on heightened self-awareness and encompasses morals and ethics; balance; relationships; positivity and openness.

When you are 'authentic' you are more likely to experience 'flow', that state of being in which something 'just feels right' (what you are doing, how you are doing it, who you are being). You will be attractive to current and potential followers (employees, colleagues, stakeholders, clients), and attract more opportunities to be yourself, as leader, in many different contexts.

When you are 'inauthentic' you will spend more time looking over your shoulder, correcting errors, the moment-to-moment feeling will be empty, dry, shallow (what you are doing, how you are doing it and who you are being is not wrong, but 'just feels off- beat'). You are unlikely to secure long-term followers, those who are following you are more likely be obliged to comply.

So being authentic seems obvious, a no-brainer – but it may be daunting. Where should you start?

Throughout your career you will have learned skills and techniques, accumulated knowledge and experience, and read widely. Consciously and unconsciously you will have observed your family, your peers, your teachers, your managers and leaders. Add to this all the things you have noticed about people in public leadership roles, gurus, the inspirational ones, your heroes (real and fictional) and you will have a wealth of resources and reference points at your disposal.

Have you become a blend of this collection of insights? What, then, is the authentic version of you? Irrespective of how much or little you have collected in the way of resources and reference points, one thing is fixed and certain: your origin, your source. This is not a place, your parents, nor the year of your birth. Your origin is the well from which authentic spring water continually flows.

Your source is what is inside you, meaning your instincts, your intuition (tuition that is 'in'). It is your flowing well of guidance, sometimes clear in words or pictures, sometimes more vague, a feeling.

The ambiguity and 'fluffiness' of this topic means that some put it down, ignore it or even deny it. But there it remains, that quiet voice inside, the nagging urge, doubt, idea, desire that, every now and then, you hear.

The more you tune into this voice, the easier it becomes to tune in, and the more clearly you receive your intuitive clues, nudges and sense of what's next. This will shift your beliefs to a 'knowing', a greater sense of certainty about who you are and what you are here to do.

'Authenticity tuning' can become a regular practice for you, not a once-a-year retreat (although don't dismiss that idea too). Find a time and a place where you can be away from disturbances (people, technology, media and so on) and ask yourself one of the following authenticity-sourcing questions, or a question of your own:

- What do I want?
- What do I want here (your role, your company, your project)?
- What feels right?
- What feels awkward or off centre?
- What's next?

If it helps, write down your dialogue and insights, no matter how vague they are. At first, it doesn't need to make perfect sense. You are just tuning in. Like a radio finding a frequency, it will be crackly until your learn how to turn the dial in subtle ways.

Start by doing this once a week, for as long as you can sustain (initially 20 minutes, extending to an hour with practice) until it has become a habit, then shift to doing it every day.

Any time you choose to invest in your authenticity will be worthwhile. One of the fundamental roles of a coach is to work with clients to help them return to their authentic state and behave, think, decide and act from there. This support may be the right option for you on this topic.

Everything and everyone you have encountered on your journey so far, all the people you will meet and the experiences you are yet to have, add to and expand your talents, allowing you to finesse the way you communicate and operate and, with it, enhance your authentic impact.

3. THE BIG

I AM

There are few phrases as powerful, as evocative, as: "I am..."

People need to understand, clearly, who you are and how you operate in order to follow you, to advocate your work and to support your leadership vision. As leader, your role is to provide a clear and consistent message to follow.

When I first meet a coaching client I often invite them to complete a few "I am.." exercises, as it tells me a lot about their attitude, self-belief, expectations and aspirations.

"I am..." is a verbal tool through which to enhance any aspect of our circumstances, feelings and experiences. Only humans are able to do this. Every time you use the term and follow it with something that is negative, you disrespect yourself, and diminish your personal power.

Who you are is something so much more powerful than most of the "I am..." statements you may be using day-to-day.

"I am..." reflects, or sets the tone for, the activity of your life. When you say and feel "I am...", you release unstoppable responses from within.

I implore you to stand guard over your use of this phrase:

"I am not..." throttles the greater potential that lies within you. There are proverbs in almost every language and culture that broadly state "everything changes for the weak person that says 'I am strong'."

I prefer to think of Rene Descartes' famous quote as "I am, therefore I think." What you are 'I am-ing' underpins all subsequent thoughts and it works with lightning speed!

The moment you entertain any type of doubt, doubt is given explicit permission to enter, and more doubt rushes in. It is the same with "I am...". Wherever you place your attention invites more of the same to rush in.

Review and refresh your "I am..." statements, for example:

"I am... free."
"I am... resourceful."
"I am... happy."
"I am... fulfilled."
"I am... prosperous."

Observe your "I am..." sentences; notice how you feel a few minutes after articulating a positive one, and then after a negative statement. Stop using this tool poorly by confirming an unwanted state with an "I am..." State the positive and allow positivity to rush in.

Your obedient servant, your brain, goes about proving your "I am..." is true, or finding proofs that it is becoming so.

4. Write it down

At some level, you know that writing is a powerful tool that more than records thoughts and facts; it significantly enhances reflection and can stimulate insight and problem-solving areas of the brain, yet most people rarely allow themselves the space to work with this incredibly simple personal development technique.

This Impact Note seeks to alert your inner mind to consider the drivers and purposeful intent in your life. What is that you want to communicate to the world? What is your purpose? As you become increasingly clear about where you are going, the clarity of purpose which you can inspire in others also extends.

How many times have you had a thought, an idea or remembered something about which you'd been racking your brain, only to forget it again within hours or even minutes? If only you'd written it down! How often have you scrawled in your notebook during a meeting or when listening to a talk and felt the same spark of inspiration and sensory memory when you glance at those notes again?

Effective leaders grab hold of such moments of inspiration, capture these and apply them. I have also observed that leaders with impact have a closer connection with their inner guidance and intuition.

The act of writing is more powerful than you could possibly believe. Across the world, neuro-researchers are discovering many brain and body links that occur when you are writing, way beyond the basic act of putting words onto paper. For example, you 'hear' and 'feel' almost everything you write, engaging with the content in multi-sensory ways.

Writing or 'interior monologue' was described as a "stream of consciousness" by philosopher and psychologist William James in The Principles of Psychology (1890) (see Further Reading on page 161). And in my work, I am frequently reminded of the incredible simplicity of this personal growth technique "to depict the multitudinous thoughts and feelings which pass through the mind", as James describes it.

When you write about one subject for a short period of time, or about all the things that occupy your thinking at a particular moment, you move past the hard-working (do-do-do) beta brain waves into alpha brain waves (where you can think more slowly, expansively and around subjects) and, with repetition, occasionally move on to the theta brain state (where you access your deeper-held and quieter instincts, intuitions and guidance).

You may be so busy, so chock-a-block with concentrating and attending meetings and churning emails that you have no time to write. Only with deliberate and determined action can you drive change here. I challenge you to try intuitive writing and make the technique work for you straight away.

Over the next week try to carry out as many 15-minute writing sessions as you can. Perhaps set yourself an achievable (and specific) but stretching goal (for example, 20 sessions, four per day, in your working week). Here are some simple tips to help you get the most from the exercise, fast:

- Take (and drink) a glass of water while you are in your writing zone.
- Write by hand (your relationship with your hand-written words is significantly different to your relationship with words you type).
- Begin by writing whatever you feel like writing.
- Write fast (let go of your judgements about quality, layout, typos and grammatical excellence).
- When you get stuck or slow down, write the question that seems to be about where you are stuck (for example when you get stuck you might write about being stuck, such as... "I'm not sure what to write now, but the question still rolling round my thoughts is which of these choices has greater potential.")
- Don't use 'yes/no', 'why' or 'when' questions – they restrict your thinking. Instead, inspire your thoughts with 'what...'
- At the end of your writing session, put your pen down, don't read what you have written, return to it later if you want to, although it is not necessary to do so.

Deep inside yourself already reside many of your answers; writing is a simple gift at your fingertips. Go on, write...

5.

'VACUUMIZING'

There is a physical law – 'nature abhors a vacuum' (or Horror Vacui as Aristotle called it in his *Fourth Book of Physics*, detailed in Further Reading on page 161) – that works just as well in everyday life as it does in creating a scientific vacuum. Where a vacuum exists, new things are drawn in rapidly.

When your world becomes overloaded, crowded, back-to-back with meetings, in-boxes full to the brim, there is no space for anything new to enter, no matter how positive your thinking may be. My challenge in this Impact Note is to experiment with the creation of a vacuum.

Leadership is not about constant activity; truly effective leadership needs space to develop clarity. Your plans, projects and goals for yourself and your team can only become clear if you create the space in which to think. Without space, there is no place for new ideas.

In your business or personal life there will be situations, clients, relationships, physical things to which you cling, perhaps you have held on to these for a long time but when you explore their value, the truth is they no longer serve you, are not part of the future you deeply wish to create, or are not creating the desired impact.

Through releasing these, you will create a vacuum into which new, exciting things will quickly flow (in alignment with the quality of your current thinking, so you'll need to work on that simultaneously).

For example:

On a practical level, you can experience the power of this strategy in your bedroom. Stand in front of your wardrobe and work the 'Pareto maxim', which states that you probably wear 20% of your clothes 80% of the time. Clear out your wardrobe. Create the vacuum. Be ruthless. Your wardrobe will resemble a pruned tree at first but give it time and wait for the results and, as for the tree, new strong vibrant branches will burst through! You will welcome into your life an updated wardrobe that matches who you are now. A by-product of this process is that someone else down the line may benefit from your clothes clearance. The same principle could be applied to your email-inbox and all those 'just in case' folders housing reference emails.

Some years ago, I had a one-day-a-week client project that had been in place for a while. It brought in great revenue, but it drained me. My work with them had nothing to do with my purpose, my future, or intentions (for my coaching business). I was only holding on to it for the money it brought in. Tactfully and responsibly I declined the project and stepped away, while my panicking ego screamed about the income I was waving goodbye. In the hours that followed, I experienced moments of euphoria, liberation and space.

In the days that followed all sorts of things happened – new meetings and conversations that led to new clients, being offered a partnership in a company and new projects. The difference this time was that I had a choice and followed my aspirations and intentions, in alignment with the impact I wished to cause and the true direction of travel I wished to follow.

'Vacuumising' could be a useful strategy for you two or three times a year; start one now, your wardrobe, your emails, your office and desk, your team, your project list. In fact, anywhere that feels full.

6. FIND THE FEAR AND DELETE IT ANYWAY

Fear can prevent you from taking action and saps the enjoyment and fulfilment from almost anything you do. It can also cause your leadership impact to become dubious, static or, even worse, damaging. But where does that fear reside, what can be done to reduce, or even remove, its overpowering effect? This Impact Note tackles the fear factory.

Personally and in dialogues with clients, I have learned again and again about the unwelcome, and sometimes unnoticed, impact of carrying fear around with you.

Not real fear, such as a 'right now' threat to a situation or to a person, but the overwhelming, poorly-defined, non-specific fear that triggers fearful thoughts, doubts, concerns, and saps empowerment, leading to overly cautious, fearful, hesitant actions and behaviours. Often the fear can be so pervasive and ingrained that you carry it around with you for hours, days and weeks.

I'm referring to fear that grips and possibly paralyses you, preventing you from making clear and confident decisions; this fear is rarely, if ever, anything to do with 'right now', this moment. It simply does not reside here. If it did, you would use your brilliant, resourceful nature to tackle it.

The disabling fear I have noticed in the most senior leaders with whom I have worked and with clients of all levels across organizations, can be worked through, and sometimes very quickly. Once it is eliminated, you will experienced waves of euphoria, bursts of confidence and doubt-free decisions. With just a few habit shifts you will learn to recognize the initial symptoms of fear looming on the horizon early on and take action before it takes hold.

The fear to which I am referring is 'over there'. It is not about now; it is fuelled by possibility, ambiguity, doubt and negative 'what-ifs'. It takes energy from the past, confirming, comparing and proving its case. This mix of past and future thinking can dupe you into believing it is more real than it actually is. It is not real, it is not here.

SIMPLE FEAR-FINDING PROCESS:

1. Become aware of fear
2. Face the fear
3. Act in spite of the fear

Here are a few laser questions to calm the fear storm early:

- **What do I fear?** Make a list, add to it with any clarity you can summon, there may be a few dormant fears, legacy fears, inherited fears, situational/trend fears (everyone has them, perpetuated and fuelled by the media, by social networks and gossip.)

- **What is true?** What is actually true about this story, not an opinion, not a likelihood, just an unequivocal truth right now? How do these truths apply or guide me today?

- **Where am I now?** In relation to the fear (that is over there) where am I now? What can I change now or stop doing or start doing that diminishes the fear? What is true now that negates the fear? Find as much evidence as possible that disputes the fear.

- **What do I want instead?** What do you want to be thinking about? What would be better? What could be different?

Just accepting and knowing that your fear is 'not here' can be liberating on its own; add that to returning your focus to now and you will notice your power returning.

7. ARE YOU SUCCESSFUL YET?

A common goal in coaching, business planning and creating career development plans is 'success', in some form or other, increasing incrementally. If goals remain ambiguous then there is a risk that nothing will ever actually feel good enough and the 'success' you want will continue to elude you. Add to this, a few tough months or a difficult environment and you may experience feelings of listlessness, even pointlessness, and you may begin to feel increasingly concerned that your business or career progress is faltering.

I often remember a coach of mine challenging me and saying over and over, "be specific". It is such a powerful coaching clarifier and might be just what you need to transform a bland and insipid definition of success into something meaningful and achievable.

Specifying success has two aspects – the sensory part (getting your senses involved) and the focus part (areas of your world upon which it is worth focusing).

Look ahead to a point in the future (such as this time next year). What would greater success feel like? What would it look like? And what would people be saying about your success? In the following five foundational areas:

1. **Work** – what you do, what you achieve, the impact of your commercial activity

2. **Personal growth** – who have you become, what has changed about the person you are and how you go about everyday life

3. **Wealth** – your relationship with money and your financial freedom, your broader wealth (beyond possessions)

4. **Health** – your body, your physical and mental capacities and capabilities

5. **Friends and family** – your relationships that support and nurture you, the impact you have upon the people in your life

Leadership, and the visible nature of your work, your visual appearance and presence, always benefit from a review of your direction and a chance to "be specific".

Write down your specifics and perhaps use this as a working document for a week (no more) and revise and finesse this as you wish. Your final version then becomes your new, clear destination, impacting consciously and unconsciously, supporting and informing your everyday choices and priorities.

And, of course, whatever you specify, always keep it simple.

8. TURN DOWN THE DOWNTURN

In the words of Shakespeare's Hamlet, "there is nothing either good or bad, but thinking makes it so." This has become a central tenet of my work – begin with the attitude that everything is neutral; from there you can exercise choice.

Your habitual (and often unconscious) good/bad interpretations make things feel as if they are the absolute truth, whereas, in fact, they are what you have decided them to be.

In the midst of a tough economic period, the coaching, facilitation and spoken word work I had enjoyed with one client company effectively ceased. Disaster! Panic!

Or... it is a nudge to shift my business focus, explore new paths, and complete my book; to stop idling and make a start on my plans for the future, to alter my brand and business focus.

I recall it being difficult at first, but this approach kept me in neutral instead of hanging my head low and feeling despondent. In fact, I have succeeded in shifting my business focus, I completed my first book, *The Simple Way*.

You have enormous power at your 'thinkertips'; as long as you are willing to do the work to become consciously aware of what your mind does, you can use it, deliberately, to shift any and all of your daily experiences.

A great way to start your change journey is simply to monitor your current 'good/bad' interpreter for a week.

At the end of each day make a note of the events (meetings, conversations, other occurrences); identify the events you felt were 'good' or 'bad'. When the day's list is complete, read through it again and challenge your own thinking (a colleague could help here to ensure you gain neutral opinions). Find the neutral, the real truth in situations. Notice how your emotional connection to the events lessens.

This process slowly convinces your mind that you have the choice. Your brain may initially resist such a challenge, but if you can see this through, I promise you will never go back!

9. GOAL-SETTING HEALTH WARNING

Goal-setting and goal-getting are trendy concepts, the stuff of champions and superheroes, aren't they? Having goals, talking about them, aligning resources around them and displaying focus on them can have immense impact and are powerful leadership activities.

Setting goals can elicit much-needed clarity and focus, and be an amazing driver of decisions and single-direction action, but there is an inherent risk in goal-setting that can be self-defeating and actually limit goal achievement, of which most people are unaware.

There is a subtle suite of thoughts, potentially simple steps you can take to heed and avoid the risk inherent in goal-setting and ultimately achieve your desired results faster. This applies whether you are a rapacious goal-setter, an occasional goal-dabbler or even an out-and-out goal-avoider.

THE RISK

Goals, by their nature, are set as a description of some kind of target future state. They represent an improvement, a change, a shift, an acquisition, a disposal. In the instant your goal is established, the energy and chemicals released in your brain and around your body are often linked to disappointment with your current situation (in comparison to the goal), impatience (with the fact that the goal state is not here yet) and imbalance in your present focus (mentally shifted to the future and away from 'now').

Any combination of these unconscious, unintended attitudes can slow you down, cause dis-ease and make the journey to the goal full of, and requiring, 'grunt and grudge'. The more seductive your goal, the more you detach from the present moment. Why on earth would you design a development journey with all that in it?

A MORE IMPACTFUL WAY OF GOAL-SETTING

Having set your goal, your desired state, whatever it is, pause. Yes, pause, do nothing, leave it there for a few minutes. Begin again by thinking through (and writing down) the following:

- What is true right now that will also be true when the goal state has been reached?
- What evidence (however small) exists now that I have the resources (or access to resources) to reach the goal?
- How will I feel when the goal is achieved? Could I feel that now in a tiny way?

This approach feels better (all the time), works faster, is more fulfilling, often even more rewarding (you will notice new results that may not otherwise have been spotted) and, in effect, you become conscious of, and open to, all sorts of other 'on-the-journey' benefits.

You may, at first, think it is too easy and the feeling state is too 'nice' meaning that you haven't performed the exercise well enough, or made it hard enough. Cut yourself some slack, allow things to be easier and simpler than you expect!

Two principles that have served me well throughout my life as a coach and mentor are "you get what you think about, whether you want it or not" and "you only get more of what you've got already."

Keep it simple and start from here, everything you need is much closer than you think!

10. THE VALUE OF YOU

At various times, I have become introspective and questioned the value I bring, particularly when at a low ebb, doubting my own value; conversely, in times of 'high flow' I have become dizzy with my own presumed brilliance. With hindsight, in both scenarios, I was missing the point.

The value you think you add may not actually be the value people gain from interacting with you. So when you hit the troughs you will not notice the important role you are still playing for those around you. When times are tough, your view will distort further.

Not understanding your mission clearly, what you bring to the table, your impact, leads to a tough journey: trying, doubting, proving, justifying. The absence of quality feedback (which evaporates in tough times) compounds your doubts further.

Your success grows and accelerates in perfect correlation to the value you add in all the environments in which you operate.

Knowing to a deeper and clearer degree what your real value is makes it easier to add more value, it becomes easier to eliminate doubt, easier to realign and find other places where your impact is truly valued.

When you find your own value, with significant ease, you can raise your game, deliver more of it, to more people, and whatever it is you deeply desire (money, recognition, respect, impact) accumulates.

To identify your own value ask (and, for full effect, write down);

What problems do you solve?

It will not be the obvious things. Sometimes, you will be solving problems people already have, sometimes it will be preventing a future problem occurring. Consider what is different as a result of your involvement, your questions, your way of doing things, how you move people or inspire them to behave. Ask people close to you. Ask trusted clients.

And if you are looking for ways to grow beyond your current role, consider (and ask) what problems those around you have that are unsolved, aggravating, disabling. You may find many new situations that you know you can do something about and add the value of you!

Of course, this same line of enquiry applies to your team or your entire company. Business 101 perhaps? Above all, keep it simple.

11. ARTICULATING YOUR VALUE

Finding powerful, positive, inspiring words and statements about yourself, your purpose and your personal brand can often be challenging and frustrating. This Impact Note outlines a method of discovering new words and phrases which can uncover and clarify the impact you have on others.

This applies particularly if you are ready for a career shift and change, perhaps towards a leadership role. This is going beyond the essential compilation of your CV or resumé to find ways of articulating, more profoundly, what you are all about, what value you add (currently or the value you aspire to add) and the impact you would like to make on teams, customers, companies and markets.

Here is a quick and simple process for getting nearer to describing your purpose and heightening the impact of the words you use.

1. Make a list of the brands, companies, products or people that inspire you, to which you feel affiliation, respect or admire.

Don't over-think the list, just note the first five to seven that come to mind. For example, when working this through with a client, their list included Apple, Bodyshop, Harrods and Richard Branson.

2. Next to each brand or person, write down what it is, specifically, that you like, admire or respect about them. My client listed against her brands/people: Fresh and constant flow of ideas; independent thinking; creating a good experience; communicating and delivering quality experiences; assisting in informed choices; confronting conventional thinking. Excellence in a few crucial areas.

3. The third step is to ascribe these comments to you, your brand, and your way of working. Take the statements on, as your own.

What you notice about others (companies or people), what you are drawn to, what stimulates your creative subconscious, is simply a reflection of a part of yourself, which perhaps lies dormant, unarticulated, awaiting activation.

In essence, you are 'borrowing' the phrases and trying them on for size. In following this process, my client moved from half-articulated descriptions of who they were to attributing a new set of attributes to themselves, attributes that felt good, aspirational, yet still authentic and truthful.

Even if career change is not on your agenda, reflecting on your purpose and journey remains a powerful exercise (and sometimes to notice the gap between who you aspire to be and the version of you that is out there in your current situation).

12. YOUR PERCEPTION - TORCHBEARER OR PROJECTIONIST?

We have convinced ourselves that our perception is like a torch that reveals a truth, when in actual fact, perception does most of the work to create a truth, rather than illuminate what is there already. It becomes more of a projector playing a film reel than a light shining on what is out there.

As one of my heroes, the late best-selling author and motivational speaker, Dr Wayne Dyer said: “If you change the way you look at things, the things you look at change!” (If you are interested to find out more, see Further Reading on page 161.)

The lesson in this has inspired me over and over again to change the way I look at things; no surprise, the picture began to shift and reveal itself differently (much more pleasantly too).

Are there situations, relationships, places in your world that don’t match up to what you really want? Maybe they have even led you to become disappointed, frustrated, tense, anxious, and angry about them.

Once you are in this place the reticular activating system (RAS) in your brain gets to work to focus only on evidence that whatever you have set to be true is true.

What you have understood to be the torch has instead become the projector, playing its film, setting out on screen your predetermined images, and filtering out the rest.

You will, quite brilliantly, find more and more fuel for your fire, grinding yourself ever more deeply into an unhelpful, potentially damaging, state and attitude.

Immediately review all the areas in which you do not like what you see. Ask yourself the question (and write down your answers for maximum effect):

- How else could I view this situation?
- What else might be true?
- How would I really want to view this situation?

Work to find evidence that your alternate viewpoints are partially true as well.

Repeat this every hour for a day, then three times a day thereafter.

Things will begin to change, people will begin to surprise you, situations will become easier, clearer and a way ahead will open up.

For an even deeper fix here put yourself in situations, conversations, places where the alternative view is more likely to come into focus. Change the way you look at things and watch them change too!

13. THE PERFECT CONSULTANT

Whatever your life, career or business situation, input from a valued, experienced, knowledgeable consultant will always be helpful. This is particularly true in the life of a leader, often seen as an isolated figure, keeping their inner concerns quiet and rarely seeking counsel or sharing with those around them.

But who is that perfect consultant, where do they reside, how can you contact them, and would they be willing to consult on your situation?

The answers to these questions lie closer than you might think.

The potential perfect consultant for you and your circumstance is... you.

Potentially.

Inspiration comes from within; insight, from within. Investigation, introspection, inklings, invention, influence, incentive, and most pertinently, intuition, all from within (big clue is the 'in' bit!).

Warning: a consultant who is negative, asks poor questions, or simply spouts opinions is soon ignored and their advice is given little or no consideration. They are insulting rather than consulting! If this is your current version of personal consulting then it is no wonder you find yourself unfulfilled, searching the world for better, more accurate and reliable advice.

The Perfect Consultant (you) may well require some skill evolution. Here's one upgrade idea that will have incredible impact on the consultant's performance:

UPGRADE THE CONSULTANT'S QUESTION

Many of our self-posed questions begin with "why...". This provokes a "because...", justifying response, and rarely leads to new or creative input. Stop "why"-ing.

Begin your self-posed questions actively with "what..." or "how could...". These questions create space for your brain to source its own answers (inspirationally, intuitively – from within).

For example, after any encounter, event or situation that went well or badly, instead of grumbling, "why did this happen?", ask:

"What could this teach me?"
"What do I want to do with this outcome?"
"How could I use this event to help me?"

Ask the questions and allow the 'in-consultant' to respond. For best effect, make notes of his or her suggestions and review later – they always come up with stuff, you could even book regular consulting sessions with them!

APPETITE:

THE ALLURE OF YOUR MESSAGE

"WE ARE WHAT WE REPEATEDLY DO. EXCELLENCE, THEREFORE, IS NOT AN ACT BUT A HABIT."

Aristotle

A DEFINED PURPOSE AND AIM IS ATTRACTIVE AND POTENTIALLY ALLURING. DEVELOP YOUR VISUAL BRANDING AND PACKAGING TO ENCOURAGE APPETITE FOR YOUR IDEAS AND SPARK ENTHUSIASM AND INTEREST IN THOSE AROUND YOU.

14. CLOTHES LINE

Your appearance acts as an outward symbol of your brand, has undeniable impact, and can be a reflection of your inner state of mind. Your appearance is your packaging and acts as part of your presence, and it does matter. It is the first method of communication with anyone new and can be the most significant way to communicate many messages, non-verbally, and show that you mean business.

Research has found that 80% of communication is non-verbal, but what many people fail to appreciate is the role clothing plays in non-verbal communication. Your clothing has an impact on the way your words are interpreted; clothing can suggest congruence, integrity and underpin or counter what you are saying.

As an example, let's say you are pitching to win an audit or compliance account for a large multi-national and your pitch is: "We are more accurate, pay greater attention to detail and we look after the small things." Yet you turn up for the meeting with a button missing from the cuff of your suit, your tie is too short, wearing odd socks and scuffed shoes. The integrity of the message is impacted by the congruency of the words versus the clothing because your clothes do not say "accurate, attention to detail and looking after the small things."

Consider your colleagues at work and how they dress, how they present themselves. Think of those who are always 'well turned out' with a tidy haircut, well-presented outfit, clean, smart shoes, attention to detail in accessories (be they briefcase, phone, handbag, cuff links, or jewellery). What does their appearance say about the way they operate? Is it consistent with who you know them to be? What assessments have you made about them, waiting to be proved right or wrong by your subsequent interactions with them? What you choose to wear is not right or wrong, it is simply an aspect of your impact.

Now consider those for whom the details of their appearance seem less important. They are, perhaps, regularly unshaven, they carry a bag overflowing with papers, they always look tired, drawn and flustered. What does this type of visual appearance say about the way they work? Such conclusions may not be true, of course, but what is interesting is the strength and pervasiveness of the first perception, which is then confirmed (or countered) by subsequent action, words or behaviours.

Appearance might not matter to you, but all sorts of subconscious flags are raised if you turn up looking bedraggled and messy. Your work may be precise and effective, but how do other people know that? They will only follow a leader who seems to have charisma and appears to be effortlessly effective, a person whose outer packaging is consistent with their message – so show them that person.

How do you come across on first meeting? You may not notice the stain on your blouse from your working lunch, or the comedy cuff links your brother-in-law bought you for Christmas, but other people might, and they will be collating that data, along with everything else. The suit you were proud of two years ago has lost its shape and you've been meaning to have a haircut since last month. You may forget, or give only cursory thought to these external markers, but to someone who doesn't know you, they are pieces of evidence that inform who you are, how you operate, and how you relate to others. The unconscious decisions those you meet are making when they first encounter you are misaligned to your impact and therefore detract from your impact.

Having an impact doesn't mean obsessing about every tiny detail of your demeanour, but do think about how you appear to others – what are the messages you emit on a daily basis? If these signals are consistent with who you are, where you are and where you want to be, then great. But it's worth taking a little time to evaluate your impact in the world, just to check that it is aligned with your intention.

If you simply re-organize your wardrobe, sort out your clothes and wear only outfits that match, suits that fit properly and shoes that are clean and presentable, the effect is immediately noticeable. Start with this, or define and accept that what you wear is part of your brand, be it pinstripes or Hawaiian shirt.

As you evaluate your current personal impact, it is easy to become bogged down with right or wrong, or judgements about others and their impact. Impact is not a value judgement, it is about aligning the impact you have with your desired outcome with more certainty over who you are, what you stand for and where you are headed.

If you are an artist, then a particular lexicon of clothes, style, culture and conversation is required, none of which is rooted in a necessity to conform to norms, to be neat and tidy or to be particularly 'productive' or 'efficient' in an economic sense. All your visual choices are whatever you have chosen them to be, as long as the message is consistent with your intention in the world.

If you want to be seen as an effective manager of a successful business, then perhaps ditching the comedy cuff links, shining your shoes and getting a haircut will communicate this more obviously to the world. Make-up, no make-up, clean-shaven or designer stubble, are all good, there is no right or wrong, but you need to ensure that what you want to communicate to the world is what is actually being seen. If these details are not aligned to your message then you are sabotaging yourself before you have begun to embark on any relationship, and you will need to expend extra energy dispelling the assumptions that have been drawn from the messages you send out. Save yourself the extra work. Clarify your message and communicate it simply, effectively and consistently.

Any realignment work you choose to take here also affects you. You may feel clearer, bolder, and more confident. You will probably have tweaked your wardrobe choices, perhaps had a haircut or had your business clothes dry-cleaned – whatever action you have taken will make you feel better immediately.

The impact on others, however, may take a little time to filter through. The people you see on a daily basis will undoubtedly notice a change in your mood or outlook, and in your general energy levels, although they may not express it. The real magic may happen a few weeks or months later, when your new default setting enables you to have maximum impact without thinking about it. This is the time when seemingly chance meetings or conversations suddenly begin to bear fruit; where deals come from nowhere or social contacts beget big business. Make changes now to reap the rewards in the near future.

Approach this area with the intensity you are ready to give it. Start with your impact scan, from shoes up to hair and hat, asking repeatedly, "is this consistent with who I am or who I am becoming?" So, if it's who you are becoming, check your clothes line, choose your make-up, have a shave, shine your shoes and pay attention to your visual impact!

P.S. *If you're not sure what to do or wear, what works for you and what doesn't, gain some feedback from your trusted circle of supporters. Perhaps even engage the services of a specialist in the area. You don't need to become the expert, just work with some who is – don't guess.*

15. FIFTY SHADES OF BLUE AND GREY

Getting the colour of your clothing right is one of the most underestimated aspects of addressing the impact your clothes make; people can spend thousands with colour consultants to get this right. It's more than just matching colour tones to skin colour and complexion, it has an impact that runs deeper and runs alongside 'clothing communication'. Ever wondered why politicians always wear rich navy suits? Because navy communicates authority, strength and power; it's the uniform colour for the police and underpins their position of authority.

Having combated my initial trepidation, I began to work with Andrew Field, a hugely experienced professional tailor who worked with Tom James Europe (whose clients are executives, their 'shop' being the executive's office). I learned so much from him in such a short period of time, it was a no-brainer to include some of his inspiration in these Impact Notes.

Andrew's helpful ideas regarding colours in suits and business wear:

- Soft mid-greys are colours to be worn when delivering bad news or when building relationships, they make us look more friendly and approachable.

- Dark charcoals communicate experience, they make us look older and 'more serious'.

- Light-coloured, rich blues make us look younger, more vibrant and fun.

Clothing impacts our everyday life, it can dictate the way we feel, the way we perform, what others think about us and what we think about ourselves. It can open doors, provide opportunities, affect our careers, love lives, relationships and the words we use. We wear clothing on the outside but it's connected to our inside, our character, beliefs, vision of ourselves and what we want the world to think about us. It may take some investment in time, thinking, advice-seeking and involve new purchases, but, done right, clothing can become an integral part of the impact you seek to make.

A good tailor will help you balance your wardrobe according to your lifestyle, work and leisure activities, so your life doesn't have to be all blue and grey. Dressing deliberately is part of the ingredients of your impact, and it all begins with colour.

16. "GOOD EVENING, MR BOND"

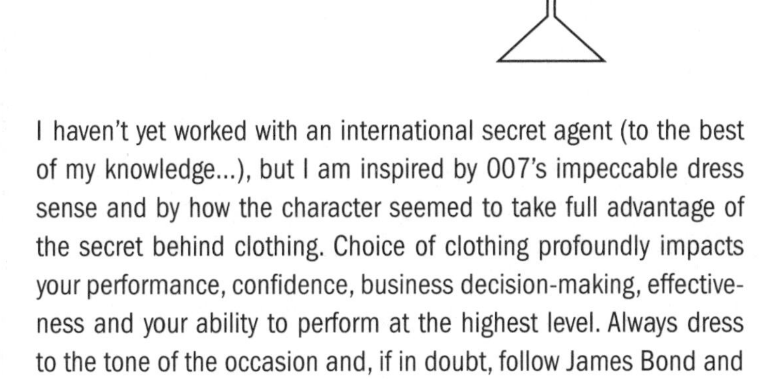

I haven't yet worked with an international secret agent (to the best of my knowledge...), but I am inspired by 007's impeccable dress sense and by how the character seemed to take full advantage of the secret behind clothing. Choice of clothing profoundly impacts your performance, confidence, business decision-making, effectiveness and your ability to perform at the highest level. Always dress to the tone of the occasion and, if in doubt, follow James Bond and dress with elegance. It's always better to apologize for being overdressed than under-dressed!

Modern society is still littered with traditional dress codes and 'uniforms' that act as golden tickets for events, societies, clubs and invitations. Consider the 'black or grey full morning dress' required for men to attend Royal Ascot and private members' clubs and restaurants that require diners to wear a jacket and dress shoes. These are non-negotiable standards for entry, dictated purely by clothing. What could be worse than being invited to an event by a client and being refused entry because your clothing lets you down?

Always check in advance, and if you don't know, ask; it's not worth losing face or a deal over a sartorial error!

Humans have an emotional connection, often unconsciously, to the clothing we wear: The quality, cut, brand and style, even the practicality and comfort. And these affect your emotions and performance too.

Whether you like it or not, the world judges you on your clothing every single day; it's commonly believed that we make our decision about people within three seconds of meeting, that's not long enough for a conversation. You are judged almost entirely on your appearance and your persona.

After colour, fabric choice the second aspect of clothing to bear in mind; this is often one thing too many for a busy executive to consider, sending them rushing off to the next retailer's hanging rail.

Finding the right fabric for the clothing in which you invest is essential to the impact you make.

For example, let's say you buy a navy blazer made from linen to attend a conference where you aim to look sharp, presentable and clean-cut; yet the properties of linen lend themselves to strength and heat regulation only and it tends to crease, look crumpled and 'relaxed'.

In a similar way, a heavy-weight woollen fabric, which will hold its shape and create a great silhouette when you are making your presentation, will fail to perform as expected if you feel the heat and this makes you, hot, bothered, uncomfortable and unable to present to your audience in a relaxed and confident manner.

To ensure your clothing makes the desired impact it is important to understand the properties and strengths of the fabric in which invest. Andrew Field's advice is that you cannot go wrong with a high-quality, mid-weight merino wool, whatever the occasion or item of clothing.

You never get a second chance to make a first impression, so looking smart with great-fitting, well-matched and co-ordinated outfits can give you an easy and tangible way of making great first impressions. The 'Mr Bond' effect runs true here also; consider how he seems, effortlessly, to win over, negotiate with and charm everyone he meets. If you look like a CEO and dress like a CEO people will more readily treat you like a CEO.

The 'power dressing' concept is widely understood, but not implemented in day-to-day life. Why reserve the feeling of elevation and confidence as well as the impact of 'power dressing' for special occasions or 'big meetings'? Don't save your best suits or clothes combos for that special event. Upgrade your wardrobe so that every day becomes a special event.

Aim to feel like James Bond every day.

17. IMPRESSING IMPRESSIONS

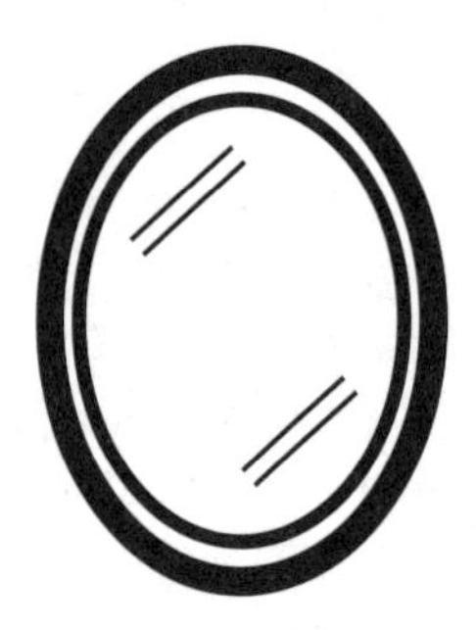

"Early impressions are hard to eradicate from the mind. When once wool has been dyed purple, who can restore it to its previous whiteness?" – Saint Jérôme (see Further Reading on page 161).

Picture the scene: Rachel arrives late for a meeting (it might be a client debrief or a first pitch). She is short-of-breath, over-heated, and shakes hands with sweaty palms. Her client is immediately thinking about the wrong things. He is preoccupied with how much time he has wasted waiting for her, rather than with the insightful report or pitching document she has written; he is thinking more about her clammy handshake and crumpled shirt, than her friendly eyes.

Before the meeting has even commenced, Rachel's client is assimilating a vast amount of information about her. She doesn't have any cash for coffee and the café doesn't take debit or credit cards. She fumbles about for a pen in the depths of her briefcase (which is overflowing with papers). She finds a flimsy plastic pen and spends two minutes furiously scribbling to enable the ink to flow.

Rachel tries to find the notes she had made on the train in preparation for the meeting, but realizes she left them on the seat with the freebie newspaper which absorbed her during the journey.

Rachel thinks all this is unimportant, that what is relevant is the work she and her team can do. She is bright, motivated and enjoys what she does. She justifies the messy details as a signal of a creative, busy mind, being someone who is 'real' rather than starchy; but, in reality, the client surmises that she is disorganized and unfocused. The client spends the first 15 minutes of discussions trying to shake off his sense of irritation about Rachel's general tardiness as it has wasted half the meeting and he needs to get back to the office to meet other deadlines.

Rachel may even give the best pitch or debrief the client has heard in a long time, but the initial impression detracts and completely negates her final delivery. The client shifts the scope, avoids commitment or simply selects an alternative supply option. Rachel takes the defeat badly, personally, at first, but on reflection finds many rational reasons to justify the lost client's choice, attributing little or no fault to her personal impact, missing the opportunity to fix and heighten her chances of future success. I observe versions of this story frequently.

How you do anything is a clue to how you do everything. The clue may be subtle and not always accurate, but to a new client or colleague, that is all they have to go on. Wisely invest time reviewing and improving your physical presence, your briefcase, your tatty old wallet or your desk environment. If you regularly go out for meetings then sit down and write a list of your 'tools' to take with you – make sure they all look presentable, consistent with the image you project, and design a system to make your meeting routine easily repeatable.

Do you need a pot of change for parking or coffees? Would it be easier to set up a tab or account at your regular meeting place to save you digging around for cash for the bill? Do you need folders of paperwork ready in your bag? A simple system can virtually automate your performance here and pay immediate dividends in terms of your personal impact.

At the core of this is defining your message. What do you want to communicate about yourself in those first few moments, or in those important everyday interactions?

Do you want to communicate positivity, efficiency, leadership, boldness, safety, caution, care, cutting-edge, certainty, inspiration, action, speed, bravery, connection, reliability, value for money, best-in-class, premium? This is not an exhaustive list, consider three or four words that appeal to you.

Now using these terms as your filters, look again at everything involved in making your first impression: your suit, shoes, briefcase. Are they consistent, do they confirm or counter your filter words?

This process can allow you to clarify where you are right now, and where you want to be. The old adage rings true that you dress for the job you want (and circumstances will conspire to make it so).

Thinking about your impact is about levelling the playing field so that your inspired ideas and productive work are met with a keen and motivated audience, ready to listen. Sort this out, and the rest will flow.

18. CONCENTRATED YOU

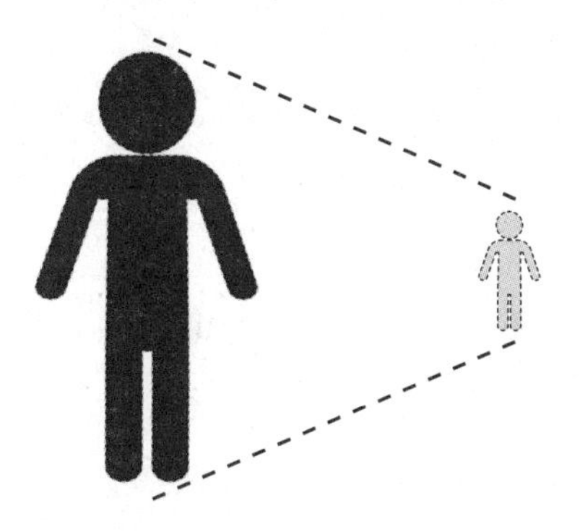

You expect yourself to concentrate and be creative and hugely productive, yet often, unconsciously, are involved in habits that directly reduce your ability to concentrate and, therefore, your impact.

In my work with clients I notice that the busier they become, the more prone they are to these impairments. Concentration becomes blocked when the demands you place on yourself increase.

How many of the following top 10 habits I have observed with clients have sneaked into your working week?

1. Becoming absorbed in games on your smart phone.

2. Turning on music in all gaps in your schedule, in the car or via headphones.

3. Scheduling back-to-back (or even overlapping) meetings.

4. Doing two (or more) things at once (writing an email, building a presentation, listening to a conference call) in the deluded hope that you are actually achieving more.

5. Taking reading material or your email device with you to the loo.

6. Working in cluttered/annoying environments.

7. Forcing acceleration in your own thinking (think, think, faster, faster), only allowing short moments for your creativity to flow.

8. Allowing distractions to take you away from 'the focused task'.

9. Taking in insufficient food and water (thirst and hunger take the brain's power away from the task).

10. Neglecting quality breathing (operating on shallow breathing for long periods).

Just noticing these things may be enough to inspire a 'me-at-my-best' scan. Consider printing out this list to stay aware and make a conscious and deliberate decision to act in a more empowered way. Eliminating the impairments one-at-a-time will deliver exponential boosts to your concentration and everyday resilience.

The simple truth about concentration is that less is more; focusing on one item and allowing the gaps to be the gaps can unleash your whole brain, and reduce stress too.

19. THE ELIXIR OF LIFE

The most essential substance we need to exist and thrive is in abundance all around us – oxygen! We have an incredible automatic system to collect it and distribute it around the body. Yet when we actually need oxygen most, and at moments when more of it would actually increase our personal capability, we unconsciously reduce its flow and make breathing more difficult. Access the 'elixir of life' and your potential increases!

In recent years I have faced some tough challenges that required me to think deeply, concentrate, and take decisive steps, I noticed dramatic change to my demeanour and vibrancy.

When you face such situations, you will have your own unconscious technique for concentrating. Whatever it is, there is a common mode that may be limiting potential every time.

Physical 'holding' and 'tightening' patterns (unconsciously holding your breath or shallow breathing, tightening shoulders or jaw) limit your potential for broad and free thinking. Consciously releasing them creates a better state of being, and, in turn, improves the quality of the outcomes and results your produce.

When you concentrate, hold your attention and focus by force, especially on difficult topics, you unconsciously install a mental 'grip', sometimes extremely tightly, and one or more of the following will take place:

- You frown
- You squeeze and narrow your eyes
- You hunch up
- Your shoulders curl forwards
- You move nearer your work (paper, book or screen)
- And in almost every person, I have coached (and studied):
- Your breathing becomes shallower.

With each one of these physical markers, you send a negative and limiting message to your team and those around you. Your physical communication to them echoes your internal dialogue. In response, they may be less inclined to contribute to meetings, to stay later in the office with you, to go that extra mile on their current project. Altering your body language is the first step to resetting your internal barometer, and is the fastest way to rescue a difficult, or potentially difficult, situation.

Number six on the list is the most restrictive item. When your breathing shortens, you trigger your body's basic functions to slow down and narrow activities to what is deemed crucial. Your emotional range reduces (from anxious, to stressed, to frustrated, and not much more), your concentration reduces (restricting creativity and new thinking), and your resilience reduces, leaving you irritable, poised to snap at any disturbance.

Whenever you notice these physical states occurring, defy them, do the opposite. Stand up, stretch, widen your eyes, roll your shoulders, and step away from your work. Access the 'elixir of life' – breathe. Take six to 10 deliberate lungfuls of air, breathing in slowly, holding briefly and breathing out slowly.

Your state will change and you will be ready to re-engage with the challenge you face. Importantly, the physical messages you are sending to those around you will lift the atmosphere and reinstate your position as a positive, inspiring, resilient, purposeful leader.

20. HUNTING HAPPINESS

You are as happy as you decide to be (perhaps contingent on your outlook, your current circumstance, your upbringing, your state of health and wellbeing and a host of other factors too). As a leader, your outward demeanor is more appealing and attractive to others if it reflects a genuine excitement or purpose. It is important that your presence communicates positivity to those around you. People will not be inclined to follow a leader who expresses gloom, despondency and lack, and even if they do they are unlikely to engage with ideas, initiatives, action and crucially, attitudes that are anything other than aligned with the leaders mode (i.e. gloom, despondency and lack).

Depending on where you fix your gaze, you will almost certainly find enough to depress you or elate you, so it's no surprise that the experience for most people is a shifting mix of both. When facilitating events, I occasionally ask participants how many days in a typical month they would describe themselves as being happy. The responses vary, are rarely towards 100%, and, more often, are nearer 50%.

This always piques my curiosity and I am motivated to increase a client's happiness ratio. There are heaps of inspirational quotes and thought-starters regarding the pursuit of happiness (and an inspiring Will Smith film of the same title).

In simple terms, happiness is a result of two things:

a) Happy incidents - these are the obvious and naturally-occurring stimulators of happiness; for example, delicious food, side-splitting humour, a loving embrace, a winning moment or securing that amazing job, contract or deal. When lots of these are in our experience, happiness seems easy. The wider the gap between their occurrence, the more effort it seems to take to be happy. Sometimes you may find yourself hunting happiness. This desire can become insatiable to the extent that even when 'natural happiness' incidents occur, they do not seem to hit home, so the hunt continues, a longing for events, people, instant gratification. It is understandable how this can become an addictive, distorted and perilous state.

b) Happy choices - the unique development of the human brain has given us the pre-frontal cortex, a powerful unit that can make emotionally-charged interpretations and decisions about anything, real or imagined, and shift our emotional state toward it, at will.

With this tool you can allow almost anything to 'make you happy'. It's a choice, not requiring any special circumstances or impetus from outside yourself. A self-sufficient happiness creator!

In practice, natural happiness may have a higher in-the-moment peak but rapidly fades, creating the craving and search for more of it.

Chosen happiness has a much longer burn and when exercised often, takes less conscious effort to create, and is easier to regulate and maintain.

Personal resilience is dramatically enhanced as your 'choosing happiness' skill grows. It will also mean that when natural happiness incidents show up, you take them in your stride in a more balanced way, welcoming them but not needing them.

This could be the most important skill to work on this year. When you decide to be happy, everything changes.

21. THE SIMPLE WAY TO BOOST YOUR CONFIDENCE

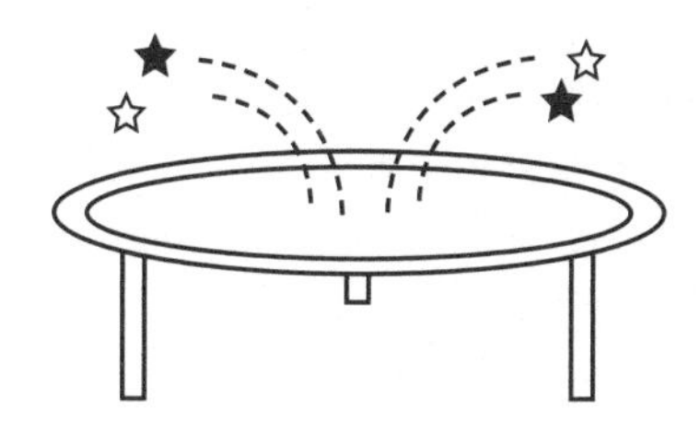

Are you a confidence player? One who needs to feel buoyant with self-confidence in order to be at your best?

The difference between your performance when confident and your performance when lacking confidence can be vast. The state of being low in confidence can be a deep pit; this Impact Note provides some steps to make the climb up and out simpler.

Many sports stars use the expression "confidence player" to describe how their performance and brilliance is significantly greater when they feel confident. Recently, I spent some time with a former coaching client who said that she had lost all her confidence, and couldn't trust herself to get back to her best.

This struck me and nudged me to look again at the distinction.

When confident you are more likely to:

- Smile
- Succeed at what you do
- Stand taller
- Take greater risks (or in some way have a healthier relationship with risk)
- Expect and act as if things will work out
- Think more freely and positively
- Have resilience against problems, conflicts and difficulties
- Make better time choices (choosing important, non-urgent life-and-goal enhancing things).
- Be less reactive

All these traits confirm, enhance and embed the state of confidence, perpetuating the empowered state.

When your confidence is low (or absent) you are more likely to:

- Frown
- Doubt yourself
- Slump and hunch (whether seated or standing)
- Procrastinate
- Expect and plan for the worst (and, as if by magic, attract situations that confirm it)
- Make mistakes
- Avoid risk
- Think negatively so that it becomes increasingly tough to 'think your way out'
- Have low resilience, be easily knocked down, swayed by naysayers and pessimists

- Make poor time choices (such as staying on the same thing too long)
- Become distracted easily

All these enhance and embed the state of low or no confidence.

So when you are confident, you act in ways that keep you confident, and when you are not confident you act in ways that keep you in that state too. You have control over both, albeit, unconsciously.

When you are in a confident state it is unlikely you will notice any drift away from confident until it is extremely obvious, when some of the symptoms in the second list are present. These, rather like a tiny leak in a dam, are seemingly irrelevant until the whole wall crumbles and the water rushes in!

Stop and review your confidence level often and take corrective or protective action immediately. I have also observed with several executive clients that the path away from the 'confident state' is a pattern. The same traits re-emerge in the same order. When you become aware of this, they become your early 'confidence slip' warning indicators.

To shift from low-to-high confidence takes deliberate, conscious and inspired action, inspiration for which is often out of reach when you are actually in that state. Waiting for some miraculous external event to make your confidence come back is futile.

Here are three important areas within which immediate and decisive attention will deliver a confidence uplift:

- **People** – list the people who are plus (you feel better, happier, focused and certain when you interact with them); the people who are neutral and negative (they leave you feeling drained). The obvious corrective action here is to reduce face-to-face time with the negatives to zero, and to increase time with the pluses every day.

- **Physical** – check and enhance the quality of your food and fluid intake (reduce intoxicants and soporific stodge, increase vitamin and water-rich foods). Consider, and take part in, the physical activity that works for you (get moving), avoid static tasks and static spans of time, stretch, pause and breathe deeply 10 times.

- **Media** – cease consuming mainstream media (TV, radio, newspaper and internet) just take in what you need for your vocation or your passion. Replace the reading time you would have used with inspirational content, articles, books, or even writing your own journal.
  Just three steps that work, every time.

This moment might not be your low ebb state. When that state arrives you may not recall this Impact Note and the simple confidence-enhancing steps so mark this page, copy it and place it behind a 'break glass in emergency' case.

22. NOTHING IS BETTER

Nothing is better – you are so busy, so full, magnetically attracting all sorts of things into the gaps in your days, without conscious choice. A leader who looks flustered and stressed sends a visual message that is far from calm and effective. This Impact Note waves the banner for 'simply nothing', which might just be the best choice you could make. Having impact is not about filling every single moment with action... your presence communicates composed, purposeful action.

Today, you are surrounded by more data-minutiae than has ever existed before. Emails, texts, social media feeds, alluring online games and apps, meetings, calls, alerts and then there is work to be done, information to read, research to be sought, conversations to be had, people to be influenced.

Finding and following your purpose and making your way through this forest of distractions is the challenge faced by everyone, but particularly by those at the top of organizations – and those with assistants who organize their diaries for 'maximum efficiency'. As you become busier, it is likely you will begin to let go of a proportion of your conscious choices about what you do, and where you spend your time. It is almost inevitable, but not compulsory.

Now, more than ever before, 'nothing is better'. Nothing could be the best choice you make. Nothing could be where you reclaim overview, your focus, your intention and your power.

Nothing is that space that is currently being filled with social media communications, gaming apps, with low-importance, low-urgency stuff.

Nothing time is that 10-minute gap between meetings where you can collect your thoughts, sit quietly and consider the focus for the rest of the day. Nothing time is the slow walk back to the train, breathing purposefully, and relaxing tension, instead of scrolling and sending messages.

- Nothing is better than playing games on your phone
- Nothing is better than reading social media on the train
- Nothing is better than reading the free newspaper
- Nothing is better than [insert your habitual time-filler]

Be proactive with your diary, book in slots for quiet thinking and planning, no matter if they are short – the benefit is positively disproportionate to the time you take, I promise, having worked this through with the busiest of leaders. Involve staff (assistants, team members) in your diary organization so that the 'nothing gaps' are not seen as unimportant; guard them carefully and you will be surprised how effective they will become.

23. DO WHAT YOU LOVE AND LOVE WHAT YOU DO

If you love what you do, your energy, enthusiasm, and passion will be infectious. You are already on the path to making an impact and leading with authenticity. If you need to find that passion, to make changes in your life, then read on; nothing changes in your life until you make a decision to change.

You may not think you have a choice about how you feel, in any given situation or circumstance, or about the role you are being asked to play right now, but you do - that is our truest and ultimate freedom.

You decide how you feel about all of it (and from that decision stems your creativity, energy, efficiency and potency... or not). Your leadership impact begins with the intent and conscious decision to communicate your energy and ideas to the world – and you can choose how you are perceived and what your purpose is.

A gift given to me some years ago was the phrase "do what you love and love what you do". This has guided many of my decisions and also the way in which I have supported others. I got to choose! This always seemed most difficult and counter-intuitive in the midst of chaos, but it was still true.

And that is the point of this Impact Note – now is the perfect time to assess what you are up to. To live the great life, to which you are entitled, everything could - and in fact it must - be in one of these two categories:

i) **What you love –** the activities that bring a smile to your face, inspire you, boost your energy, you may find them easy or not, but you definitely love being involved with them. It feels like the stuff you were born to do. If this doesn't account for a good portion of your everyday mix then work is needed here soon (dig through these Impact Notes for new thinking).

ii) **Love what you do –** everything else after number one needs to fall into this category. Even if you do not enjoy it at the moment, blissful freedom comes from finding ways to love it, no matter what. For example, stop telling yourself how much you hate the governance meetings or the ironing and pose the question in your mind "what is great about this?".

I'm not certain that there is an ideal in terms of the percentage split between 'what you love' and 'loving what you do', other than the need for the first to outweigh the second. The first will feel natural, enjoyable, and in spite of any feelings of guilt or questions about your worthiness, you will want to spend time doing these activities. In the second, it is implicit that you work on your attitude and connection to the item in question – it will demand some gentle, conscious effort. If more than half your time needs this 'gentle effort', you may feel drained. Work is therefore required to move some of these items on... delegate them, outsource them, pay someone: don't do them. And instantly replace them with category one – something you love.

24. SOMEBODY'S WATCHING YOU!

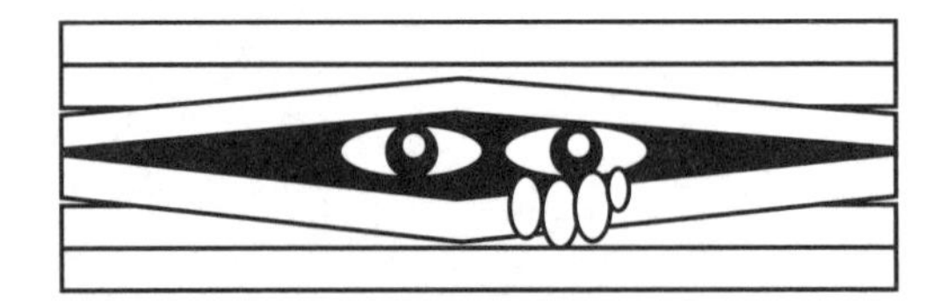

For a whole heap of reasons people around you (your followers, potential followers, your critics and questioners and the ambivalent ones) are watching you. They are noticing how you stand, how you sit and how you walk, what you say and how you say it, how you interact with others, your habitual acts, your twitches, where you show up and where you don't.

It may not be obvious; in fact, it may not even be a conscious act on their behalf. But you are in view, visually, aurally, emotionally, spiritually almost all the time; from the moment they meet you to the impact you have left several minutes or hours later.

There is a risk here that you could take this Impact Note too far and neurotically overthink the mass of elements that are involved – be gentle! All the messages you emit that are consistent will embed you brand and confirm and extend your impact. Any acts or words or behaviours that are inconsistent will weaken your message, reduce the clarity and lessen your impact.

Consistency is the goal here.

I have worked with clients on this challenge in a number of inspirational ways.

One, in particular, found an interesting way of heightening her awareness. Alison works in the city centre and had noted the huge number of CCTV cameras sited in streets, car parks, corridors and stairwells. She imagined the cameras were there to capture her movements as she went about her day. Every time she caught sight of a CCTV camera it nudged here to check her posture, raise her game and run a quick check of how she was coming across.

Another client, Graham, mentally-installed a filter for a period of a month to evaluate his choices and habits. The filter was simple: "Is this (decision, act, choice of clothing, behaviour) something that the future me would be pleased with?" This upgrading device helped Graham maintain or improve his image across many areas that could be witnessed by the people he served. For him, the most important improvements were in how and where he showed up. This included the types of comments he made on blogs, on Twitter, Facebook and LinkedIn and the images and photographs of him that were out there in the web world. It also meant he sharpened his 'away from work' image, in terms of how he dressed and behaved.

You wouldn't expect the director of a global corporation to use expletives in a slating of their favourite sports team, nor would you expect to find a photograph of her on holiday wearing a T-shirt emblazoned with an offensive image. These are extreme examples, but the point is still clear.

You are always on stage. You lead; you have impact. Be the example.

If somebody is watching you, does what they see, hear or feel enhance or impair your leadership impact?

25. GETTING RID OF THE...

Creating and expanding your sense of awe is one of the most liberating and relief-providing remedies I can prescribe to maximize your leadership impact.

When times are tough and your mood dips and you feel the pressure of concentration or just the grip of concern, your ability to notice the awesome in anything wanes. Your ego kicks in and steers your thinking, you may feel more fearful and bounce from mini-disaster to aggravating relationship to disappointing event. It is awful!

In hindsight (what a wonderful place that is) I found myself in this state at various times during 2011, slowly and almost imperceptibly becoming disconnected from the great things around me. Some years before I worked with fellow coaches Scott Wintrip and Jay Perry on the 'SimplyEffective' Coaching Program and one of their most powerful tenets was "there is an awesome in every awful!" (See Further Reading on page 161 for Scott's blog.)

Finding the awesome around you loosens the hold of the ego, staves off disaster and can liberate you from fear. It works every time. Furthermore, being in a state of awe practically removes the chances of you experiencing boredom or disappointment.

So here's my challenge...

Right now, find five natural occurrences in your daily life (that perhaps you have taken for granted up until now). For a few moments consider the awesomeness. For example, the sky, the plants and wildlife around you, the wind, rain, sun, a cobweb, grass between paving stones, the people walking by. Expand your ability to observe 'awesome' as you repeat this exercise to include anything you notice, technology, buildings and so on. Make no judgements, just capture 'the awesome'.

Return to this exercise whenever the grip of ego returns, and at least once a day. In doing so, you will not become weary, in fact you are likely to shift your energy levels significantly upwards.

This will not be an automatic thing for you to do. Your habitual mode is probably to notice the awful and then to articulate it, rue it, cuss it, in effect painting it on the walls around you. That ends up being all you see and experience, prompted again and again.

The potential for awesome becomes obscured and blocked.

It is through actively working on this Impact Note, building it into your daily practice, that you will retrain your mind's sensory radar.

Find the awesome in every one of your awfuls today.

ADVOCACY: NURTURING YOUR CHEERLEADERS

"IDEAS BECOME POWERFUL ONLY IF THEY APPEAR IN THE FLESH; AN IDEA WHICH DOES NOT LEAD TO ACTION BY THE INDIVIDUAL AND BY GROUPS REMAINS AT BEST A PARAGRAPH OR A FOOTNOTE IN A BOOK."

Erich Fromm

YOUR IDEAS AND VISIONS MEET THE WORLD IN A POTENT WAY WHEN OTHERS EXPERIENCE YOUR INSPIRATION AND BELIEVE THEY CAN JOIN YOUR AIMS WITH POSITIVE ADVOCACY. CONSIDER YOUR VERBAL AND PHYSICAL COMMUNICATION WITH OTHERS. ENCOURAGE A BUZZ AROUND YOUR LEADERSHIP AND YOUR GOALS SO THAT YOUR VISION CREATES ITS OWN MOMENTUM.

26. HOW ENGAGED IS YOUR TEAM... REALLY?

Employee engagement has become a major focus for almost all corporations.

Your team, your suppliers, contractors and resources perform better, more is achieved when they are engaged.

You must have an understanding, what it is, how to notice it, how to measure it and how to influence more of it. All this is based on the sound belief that engaged employees perform better, provide greater customer service, achieve better results, faster, are more creative and are less likely to leave.

Unsurprisingly, there are a plethora of measurement devices and surveys offering employers a robust, quantifiable engagement metric. These, at least, provide a form of comparable yardstick to monitor progress or regression. However, I have noticed, all too often, that the measured question or statement becomes the goal, and tactical initiatives are dreamed up and put in place to drive a marginal change in one or more of the metrics. There is a huge risk that the point has been lost and employers could be deluded that all is well.

At the core of employee engagement, and the most significant contributory factor to its positive state, is the impact of the leader and their leadership behaviour. Gulp.

There will be an exhausting list of basics that all companies need to have in place, or work on continuously, to ensure employees shift from disengaged to engaged. Of most interest to me is that tranche of employees considered 'engaged' and your role as their leader.

Engaged employees look engaged, behave as if they are engaged and you will feel assured that, in the main, they put in effort and do the right thing, at the right time. I have observed a further distinction between three types of engaged employees who have may, up until now, been viewed similarly. You have a role in transitioning them upwards.

Essential effort – these engaged employees are positive, involved, doing the right thing, working well and completing tasks. It's their job, their livelihood, the business requires them to behave and act this way, and they are doing it.

A team of 'engaged essential efforters' ensure the essential job gets done.

Obliged effort – these employees are active in more as edicts and managerial request are made, they use a degree of initiative and get involved, work longer, take part in peripheral committees and work groups. They seem absolutely like the group of engaged employees that every survey would love to meet and monitor. As their leader requires it, they jump. But they are not the purest of followers. They are consciously or unconsciously obliged to put in this increased effort, their career protection and progression depends upon it. Their resilience is stronger than the 'essential efforters', their instincts sharper. Undeniably they are engaged, but often purely for their own reasons (which is not a bad thing).

A team of 'engaged obliged efforters' ensures the job gets done and obvious, within limits, advancements are made.

Discretionary effort – there is overlap between all three of these engaged sub-categories and particularly between 'discretionary efforters' and 'obliged efforters', hence it can be easy to just take them all as one group. Discretionary Efforters use heightened awareness, notice what is needed or missing and step forward. They are deeply engaged not just with their role and the company but with their leader too. They are attuned to their leader, aligned with his or her vision and want to get there too. They are more likely to adopt a similar tone to their leader, and to approach things in the same way; they are already up-standing and standing firm when called. They don't necessarily work longer hours or dedicate every waking hour to their work, but they are passionate about the purpose of their role in their team – they may read or research in their own time, or spend time thinking about how to develop excellence in the product or service. They work with heart, rather than simply clocking up the hours.

A team of 'engaged discretionary efforters' will have a dramatic impact themselves, beyond results. This is a movement.

As a leader, you will already have a clear and unambiguous role in engagement (or disengagement); my challenge to you is to heighten the awareness of your engaged teams and consider the three sub-categories. As your leadership impact extends and becomes increasingly clear to your followers, you will move them through the stages.

Look again at your engaged employees and notice the efforters. Your next step in nurturing the 'discretionary efforters' is to understand your own motivations deeply and then work on communicating these, with authenticity and passion. Work through these Impact Notes to discover how your personal impact - verbal, physical - can inspire the efforters at all levels to share in your vision.

Any leader worth their salt will drive engagement. Only leaders with profound impact create teams of engaged employees whose discretionary effort creates immense change.

27. TELL THEM WHAT THEY WANT TO HEAR

The way in which you communicate with others can elicit the best or the worst from them. Everyone has their own unique set of needs and ways in which they interpret your message. This Impact Note simplifies the ways in which you can enhance that connection with everyone in your team and maximize your positive impact.

The busier you become, the less attention you may pay to the people around you, to your team or family members, and the information upon which they thrive may no longer be provided by you. If your feedback to team members is often blunt and clipped they may feel less like contributing in future. You may not realize you are communicating in this way as junior members of a team rarely voice their thoughts on such matters.

Your stakeholders, team, family or friends are frequently in need of a unique combination of the following four messages from you:

1. **How am I doing?** – are they making progress, what results have they achieved (tangible or not); challenge them, positively, to do more.

2. **Do you agree and support me?** – be positive and upbeat about your connection with them and what you do, let them speak (you need to get their thinking 'out there' in order to move on), and affirm them.

3. **Am I valued?** – praise the quality or action (rather than the person), link importance to their work, and appreciate them.

4. **Is this right?** – confirm expectations, guidelines, or rules and provide objective information - simple, clear, unambiguous - remove the rest.

When there is short supply of these or the message you deliver is not actually what they need in one of these areas, they may unconsciously begin to act differently. Some may become bullish or manipulative or retreat into their shells or repeatedly give in to arguments. Avoid reacting or responding to the less productive, changed state you observe in others and go back to this list of four. Proactively shift the time and emphasis of your messaging.

Good luck! Notice more, keep it simple and take inspired action.

28. THE GREATEST GIFT AND THE GREATEST CURSE

What you say has a significant impact on others and on you as well. You have the power to change reality.

The words you use have incredible power to ignite change or to dampen your fire; as scientists, educators, anthropologists and learned professors have said, our ability to speak is both our greatest gift and our greatest curse.

When you speak, a number of processes take place, most at a sub-conscious level. Through your words you bring into reality what previously was just a thought or idea. In simple terms, I observe three elements.

First, is the reaction to the need to speak and the sourcing of what you might communicate.

Second, is the actual construction and delivery of the words (which sometimes feels simultaneous but isn't).

Third, is you actually hearing the words you have spoken.

So everything you say has a triple recording and embedding action. And that's before you consider what others hear, believe and act upon as a result of what you have said to them, which may reinforce your words back on you.

One of the first things I notice with clients is their language, their vocabulary, tone, intonation, and specifically, the words they use to describe themselves, their situations and their current reality.

Any real, lasting change has to start with you, otherwise you actually become the resistance to the change itself by what you repeatedly say. When you speak, you describe the reality that may (or may not) have just been the case for you. More crucially, you also prescribe how it is going to be from this point on. And that simply does not have to be the case. Your words are the keynote for the next series of thoughts you and others will have.

You can shift your words, actively stating a more positive and empowered version of the truth (for example, from "I'm stuck in this role", to "I have more to learn"). Your creative subconscious goes off to find proof and to initiate new thoughts, ideas, responses, and patterns in relation to 'more to learn' as opposed to 'being stuck'. From here, your brain can gear up to move in the direction of the reality you want, rather than confirming the mire you are in. You set the direction of travel.

How do you frequently describe:

- Who you are, your health and your current performance?
- Your current challenges?
- Your company, team and work environment?
- Your relationships?
- Your finances?
- Your future?

What improved version could you use to describe and prescribe these six areas? Re-write them now and refer to your notes for a while until you repeatedly use the upgraded version.

Your words. Your reality. Your choice.

Take responsibility.

29. AMBIGUITY AND IMPACT

Today's world seems to demand that you find an answer, the right answer ridiculously quickly. Dialogues in which you are involved drive for certainty and it (the answer) often remains elusive. There is a simple way to boost your conversation skills and enhance your leadership communication with the surprising and under-used power of ambiguity and vagueness.

While it can be challenging to deal with someone who remains permanently ambiguous, vague and non-specific, there is hidden power in its simplicity and judgement-free openness; a skill very much worthy of exploration and finesse.

When I observe dialogues in today's feisty corporate situations, there is a hint of desperation in many conversations, a search for absolutes, interrogative questioning and almost imploring requests for certainty. This is true both in the request from the asker and in the meanderings of the responder. Questions become narrower and laser-in too soon. Those forced to answer wriggle and avoid commitment, where certainty is not ready to be found.

It seems counter-intuitive, but increasing the ambiguity and vagueness (A&V) of your dialogue can elicit greater input from others. The people with whom you are communicating become less inhibited by having to 'nail the answer' to an otherwise pointed question. This is a core coaching skill which can deliver benefits in any dialogue, and ironically, is often a faster way to gain clarity, as more time is given to expanding thinking before zooming in.

A&V allows the contributor to unravel an answer without fear of failure (at an unconscious level). It enhances their connection with you as they feel you are allowing them to talk and be heard (Abraham Maslow's Hierarchy of Needs theory describes the importance and impact of this 'need to be heard' in fourth level, ego or esteem).

Words to weave into your dialogue that will heighten its ambiguity, and more specifically, your questions:

- Might
- Could
- Possibly
- Maybe
- Perhaps
- Consider
- What about if
- And a catch all: What else?

When you want to bring the conversation in, rather like landing a fish that's been on the line for a while, just add the word 'specifically'. For example - "what might you do here?" becomes "what specifically might you do here" – the question still seems explorative and not directive to the receiver, but the word 'specifically' sharpens their second response and their commitment to it.

Good luck. Start with practising in safe, low-risk conversations and keep it ambiguous and simple.

30. WHERE ARE YOUR BOUNDARIES?

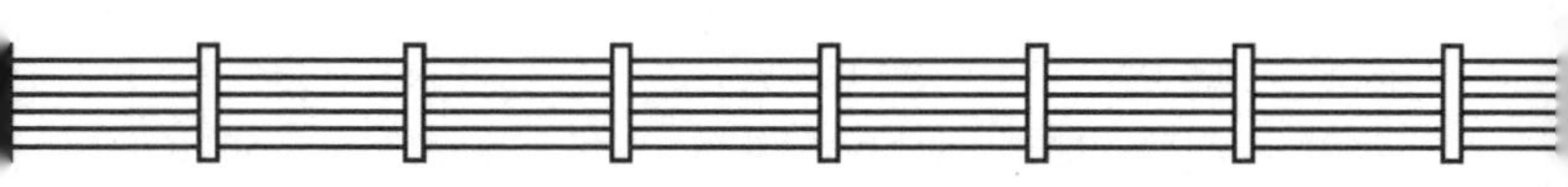

Experiencing annoyance, frustration and nuisance can simply be an indication that your boundaries with others have been reached, crossed or become blurred. Leaders who have the greatest impact are clear in their purpose and don't attempt to do everything. This Impact Note brings your focus back to re-setting boundaries that will help you and your team thrive.

Defined or undefined, conscious or unconscious, you have boundaries and everyone around you (customers, colleagues, friends, family, especially children and pets) work to them, test them and ultimately respect them in direct relationship with how you respect, honour and communicate them.

In teams, just as in families, where a boundary has been clear and consistent, they accept it and develop with it - harmony prevails. Where the boundary becomes fluffy, i.e. where goal posts within a project change frequently, or managers are distracted or busy and not focusing on specific project outputs, where standards drift (time-keeping, output and quality) boundaries can be seen as negotiable and worth testing, behaviours change and situations become fractious.

My work with clients and their teams always includes boundaries. You are likely to carry this learned behaviour with you from childhood to adulthood, seeking boundaries for what is right, expected and acceptable in almost every aspect of your life: Noticing them, assessing whether they could be or should be extended or brought in, and most of all, being consistent in their definition, considering if a particular one is actually necessary, and supporting the intent for consistent impact. Once defined, the environment becomes transformational, clear, and frequently much more enjoyable and fulfilling for everyone involved. Progress is faster, communication and expectation clearer and your impact is effective.

The more chaos you experience in your everyday activities, the more reliable a sign it is that your boundaries have lost definition.

Your boundary work:

Boundary check – where are you being called to exert more effort than feels appropriate? Where do you have to step into situations too often? Where are the interaction errors (arguments, breakdowns, disappointments, mistakes)?

Re-write, draw new boundaries, or be more determined about those about which you have become fluffy and communicate them clearly. Hold the line - you will be tested - particularly following your review and the definition of new boundaries (it is human nature to check and validate new boundaries when met).

Example areas where your boundaries exist:

- **Time**
  (starts and finishes, meetings, payments, responses/replies)
- **Quality standards**
  (setting clear expectations on volume, depth and breadth)
- **Other professional standards**
  (dress code, relationships, communication)
- **Feedback**
  (what you want and what you'll give)
- **Work ethic**
  (focus times vs interruptible times)

Review your boundaries when the frequency of challenges increases.

Start with your working days, and the time you 'finish'. Is it boundless, ill-defined? Colleagues and family don't really know where they stand while you have no boundary, and will respect your working day in direct relation to how you define your own boundary.

If you immediately feel resistance at the thought of working on the structure of your boundaries, it is likely you will feel benefit significantly from even the lightest review.

Be specific, press on.

31. BUILDING

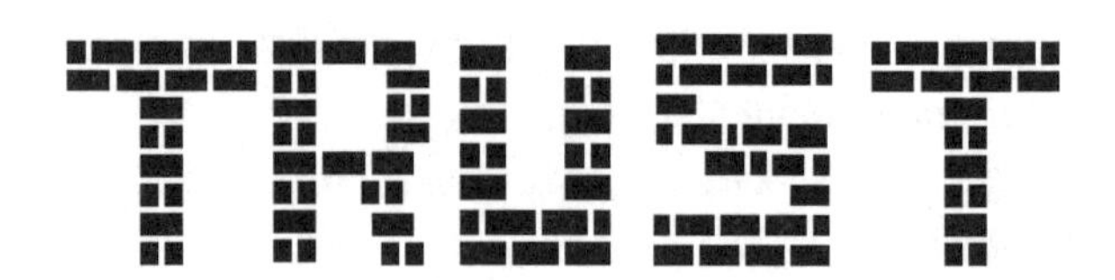

Trust is much talked about in business today. It is a core component of many development initiatives. How a company or team can be trusted, your trustworthiness, the way teams operate in high-trust or low-trust environments. The actions and behaviours you take, or your brand takes, can enhance or damage trust.

Trust is a foundation upon which much can be achieved. Without trust, the experience of working is dulled, frustrating and unfulfilling for both you and your staff or team. Where trust exists communication is easier, leaps are made in projects and tasks, ideas and initiatives, barriers and obstacles are overcome.

Books and esteemed speakers seek to make this ambiguous trait tangible, but it often remains difficult to grasp and find improvement action steps.

Do you need to shift the trust with someone in particular, or a group of people? Would the performance of your team shift if it had a stronger trust base? Does your company or brand have challenges in its market place or with its customers regarding trust? Are you seeking a reliable and effective shortcut to grow trust?

I have worked on trust with individuals, teams and entire organizations and a simple route for evolution does exist for all these situations. Much has been written about trust and the issue can become complex and laden with categories, sub-categories and a spread of contributory factors that can be focused on and turned into change initiatives (see Further Reading on page 161, which lists Stephen M R Covey's *The Speed of Trust*, packed full of initiatives and ideas and suggestions and strategies and tactics and focus groups and discussion topics).

The development of trust has two dependents (putting the 'W.E.' in trust):

- **Willingness** – the willingness or propensity of a person or group of people to trust. Some people naturally or culturally do trust, some naturally or culturally tend not to. It doesn't matter which, it just is. One group experiences many disappointments and let downs, the other always seem to be on a longer journey to achieve trust foundation.

- **Evidence** – the volume of occasions when trust becomes real, tangible action, words and results. The more indisputable and more frequent these are, the greater effect they have on the foundation and accumulation of trust.

'Willingness' is largely a given, often engrained and slow to change, you can only influence this over time.

'Evidence' is within your gift. Creating trust-evidencing events as frequently and appropriately as you can.

The simple and effective route to raising trust rapidly is:

1. Make a commitment
2. Deliver
3. Repeat

That's it. Your application of this process will work, it is as simple as that. The commitments may be small or great. You can increase your trust development speed and effectiveness by evolving two elements: relevance (of the commitment) and value (of the commitment to the other party).

You will notice a difference after just a few commitments delivered, try it and see. If you stop making commitments or fail to deliver, I suggest trust returns to its original state, or perhaps slips further back. So this trust development journey is a commitment in itself. Take the challenge when you are ready, in areas that are important for you and your evolution.

32.

No matter what decision you face, big or small, significant or irrelevant, your creative brain, an intelligent, thinking leader, is likely to continue playing with the options.

Sometimes you need a little extra deciding-cement to really make the decision and move on. It is likely that the higher the number of factors involved in reaching a decision, the greater the level of brain power that will still be at work evaluating, validating and checking your final commitment.

In that moment when you make your decision you have the power to embed it thoroughly, but this final step may often elude you.

Here's a method to enhance your decision-making in these areas (particularly useful if this 'wiggle room creativity' has become a cover for procrastination).

1. Decide – choose the option, with whatever technique or process you prefer (if it hurts and you experience significant feelings of discomfort and doubt, there is still more evaluation to be done, put down this technique and return to it later).

2. Grab a piece of paper, write your decision at the top, and divide the page into two columns.

3. In column one, list all the reasons why this is the right decision (add to this over the course of a couple of days).

4. In column two, list all the outcomes that will become possible/available as a result of your decision (add to this over the course of a couple of days).

5. Every day for two weeks read your lists (aloud if your vicinity permits).

In following this method, you will drown out the doubter and the procrastinator, reminding your creative sub-conscious of all the reasons why you have made your decision. You will have momentum. The more often you work with decision-glue, the less often you will doubt or reconsider your decisions. It just gets better!

33. LISTEN TWICE

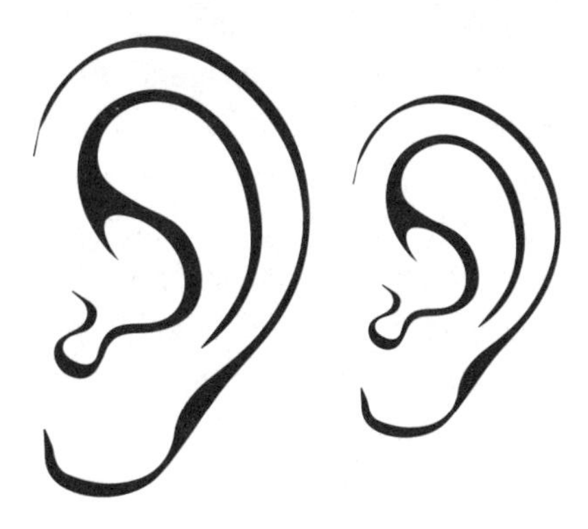

Do people mean what they say? How accurately do you hear what is actually said? Where did your thinking go while the other person was talking?

The answers to these questions can define the quality of your relationships, the extent of your influence, and the potency of your messages. This Impact Note shares a method for heightening your listening skills in every situation.

Whether you are a leader, a manager, a senior executive, creative or entrepreneur, listening skills will always be a crucial part of the influence you have and the relationships you build, and without doubt, the degree of impact you can exert.

Two simple listening truisms:

a) People rarely mean exactly what they say.
b) What you hear is more your choice and less to do with what was actually said.

Therein lies the challenge of communication. Compound that with busy environments, pressured situations, clocks ticking, demands calling, deadlines looming and it is no surprise intent gets lost, misheard, wires-crossed and breakdowns occur.

I have often worked with clients to heighten their awareness of both truisms. The quality of their communication always improves thereafter.

When you are busy, immersed in your world, it is highly likely you will fall into the opposite of the truisms, totally accepting that others mean exactly what they say, at all times, so you'll act directly in accordance with that; secondly, you will accept that what you hear and interpret is accurate and forms the basis for what you do or say next.

What lies behind these listening truths is:

1. People wrap many things in their spoken messages – subtleties, nuances, hopes, pleas, insecurities, requests, previous and future aspired-or-feared situations – all packaged and delivered consciously and unconsciously.

2. Your ability to 'hear' is inhibited by how full your head is, the conscious and unconscious biases you may have, previous-and-anticipated future situations, and your recent experiences with the person with whom you are interacting.

If you find this resonating with your experience, then consider 'listening twice'.

For a couple of weeks, especially in conversations with colleagues who are often on different wavelengths, listen twice before responding. In simple terms, hear what they say and give yourself a moment to hear it again as if it were echoed. Let your brain do the rest on its own, and it will. This replay will allow all of your repertoire of listening skills and intuition to engage and your range and choice of responses will be markedly more evolved. Keep it simple and enjoy listening twice.

34. STOP WHINING

When your situation changes and has become one that you no longer want or dislike or need to change, your frame of mind and approach becomes the most important factor for your way through. This Impact Note focuses specifically on the power of your attitude.

When working with Jon, a senior leader, I introduced a simple attitude-shifting tool to help him regain focus and shift to positivity regarding a situation, which he was not enjoying. Jon wanted to move on, out of the situation, and the more he talked about it, the worse he felt and the more difficult it seemed to become. He became quickly overwhelmed with doubt, and soon it could have morphed into despair.

Have you experienced, or are you in, a situation that just isn't working the way you want it to? The connection you have with those involved may have become poor, frayed and tense.

The three steps to move you into a better frame of mind and actually begin to create positive change take some work, but they are simple.

'Stop Whining' is inspired by my irrepressible friend Warren Creates, an international lawyer and campaigner for human rights, who displays signs around his office stating this clearly and often.

- Just stop – your whining and complaining simply regurgitates the ill-feeling, confirming your resentment and disappointment. You have control over your thoughts, so shift your focus. Your physical response will be linked to these thoughts, you will frown and slump, your voice pitch and tone will alter, also affecting the words that you speak.

- Go with the flow – allow things to be the way they are, stop resisting and pushing back, counter-arguing or challenging the current state, wishing it to be anything else. It is what it is, your resistance is only likely to compound it, not change it. This doesn't mean you are rolling over and agreeing with it, you are simply moving into a more powerful state in relation to it. The alternative perpetuates the friction.

- Be happy – with what is happening right now, all of it, whatever (this takes strong self-talk and active work noticing the good bits). Get involved in activities that inspire you, uplift your thinking. Display your upbeat attitudes, get busy. This step may take the most energy but is the step that accelerates the likelihood of achieving the outcome you really want.

Each of the three steps helps and underpins the other two, so work in one area will make it easier in the others. The outcome of all three steps is a no-brainer. Someone who no longer whines is more enjoyable to be with, someone who goes with the flow is easier to be with, someone who is happy is good to be with. Your positive impact increases dramatically.

If you chose to adopt this approach it cannot be 'partly followed'. It's an all-or-nothing decision and it requires practice to ensure you create consistency. Working on this with a colleague will heighten awareness and accelerate success (for both of you).

35. FINDING YOUR OFF SWITCH

Stress and tension are possibly a part of your everyday regime. It's been part of your make-up for such a long time you have accepted it, adapted to it and secretly even welcome it. Your entire behaviour and character has adapted to incorporate a 'normal' stress level that you have unconsciously accepted.

Without doubt, we human beings have evolved an incredible capacity to handle stress and respond appropriately (or not), driven to stay safe, cope and progress.

In observing leaders, senior executives, entire teams, fellow passengers on trains and planes and drivers in congested traffic, I see their accumulated tensions, physically displayed, possibly not noticed in themselves, just taken as being part of who they are (because they've been in stress mode for so long it has become their new normal).

Much of this tension build-up is unconscious, and unwinding is not an automatic process; as a result, you're unlikely to be employing sufficient unwinding strategies. Your main stress-reducing and tension-release method will probably be sleep, however fitful. Your morning regime though, unconsciously picks up many of the stresses again (the next day's challenges, that looming event, the unmet needs, incompletes from yesterday, your current sense of being overwhelmed).

In this Impact Note, focus on the tension itself – not the factors that have led to it.

Indisputably, when you are tense, you will be less flexible, both physically and mentally. You are less likely to experience enjoyment, to notice opportunities, to receive insights, to contemplate challenges creatively. Your tension-free state offers this potential.

Your tensions have probably been with you for some time, the longer you have had them, like barnacles on a boat, the tougher they will be to shift. And all the while they are there, like the barnacles, they will be impairing your travel, altering your speed and performance efficiency.

Sit, stand or lie in the most comfortable way you can, with your spine straight, not curved. Follow this simple three-step switch off:

1. Switch off your system, relax, and sink deeper into your stance, chair or bed. Become aware of the difference, which may be significant, even at this first stage.

2. Take a deep breath in and out.

3. Run a scan up and down your body from toes to the top of your head, does anything still feel tight or tense?

Now repeat the exercise – switch off your system again, paying particular attention to the tight or tense places detected in the first scan, and sink deeper.

Run the scan again, noticing where you feel less tense or still tense.

Repeat this process up to six times. The degree of change will, of course, lessen as more switch-offs are applied, but keep going.

Following your final switch off, take three breaths in and out, as deeply as is comfortable for you (in through the nose and out through the mouth). This retunes your body to the new reduced tension level.

Return to the day at a measured pace. Enjoy.

36. THE SHOULD SHIFT

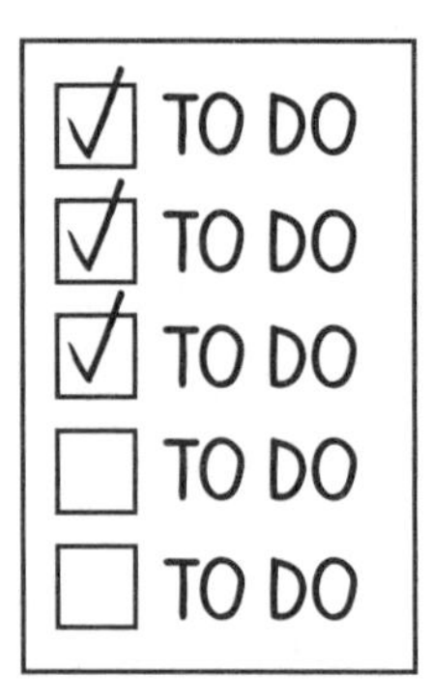

Every time you use, and particularly say out loud, the word 'should' you are setting yourself up for extended pain, reducing your own choices and forcing yourself to take action that might not even be part of your true journey.

This Impact Note provides a way of shifting to a more powerful mindset. It also reminds you that 'should-ing' your staff and colleagues often elicits a negative push-back.

I often highlight specific words that carry within them immense power; power to drive you forward or power to drive you down.

This note shines a light on 'should', which I believe is one of the more damaging words in our language when used without care.

In my 20 years as a coach, no other word has represented, more obviously, the door to unlocking barriers to change, growth and personal evolution. You may be able to hear yourself say it (or its evil partner word 'ought') and, with it, comes an almost immediate sense of disappointment, pressure, lack or even failure.

Try this simple unravelling method. You can do it alone, but the experience may be deeper and more effective with a colleague or coach.

1. First write a paragraph that summarizes your current situation; career, finances, relationships, health. Just at a general level, no need for specifics yet.

2. Next list up to six sentences beginning: "I should..."

3. Pick any three of the sentences and briefly consider (or share if you are in a group) why you should do that or be that? It is likely that what comes to mind begins to describe where you may be stuck, full of doubt or unconsciously limited.

4. Then for the 'simple shift' – go back to your list and re-write two or three of the sentences with "If I actually wanted to, I could..." Re-read them and consider your connection to that item anew; what stops you doing or being that now?

Saying 'could' (or its helpful and positive double-meaning partner 'might') creates empowered choice and removes the forcible way in which you may be approaching your 'should do' list. Perhaps you could take this exercise into your next team meeting and use it to uncover any 'should' that sits in your group or company.

"You really should take action on this Impact Note" feels like another weighty item to add to the bagful of your potential personal development actions.

Versus...

"If I wanted to, I could take action on this Impact Note" which gives you the choice, lessens the heaviness of having to do it and gets you ready to take inspired action:

"I choose to take action on this Impact Note now/tomorrow/next Monday."

37. TRUTH OR DARE?

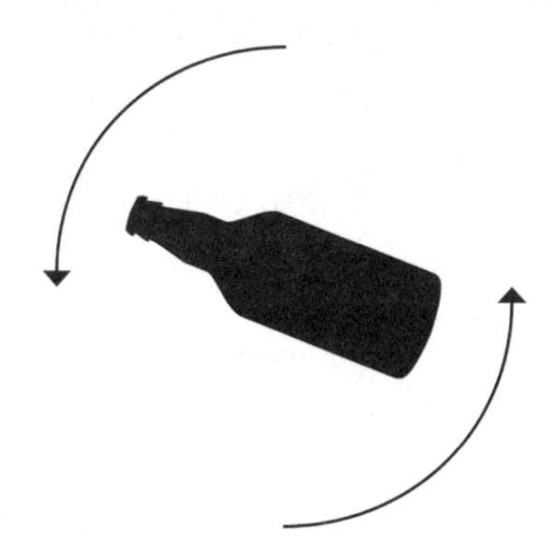

I am not overdosing on the Pollyanna principle (a term meaning positivity bias, coined from the 1913 novel by Eleanor H. Porter detailed in Further Reading on page 161), but simply challenging you to look again at your current situation and the attitude or set of beliefs you are carrying every day.

As the leader of a team or organization, your ability to create enthusiasm and commitment from others is rooted in what you, personally, believe is possible and influences the culture and attitudes of those who work with you.

During your most challenging leadership days, times can be tough. But is it really as bad, intense, busy, overwhelming, difficult, and complicated as you are telling yourself (repeatedly and often unconsciously)? It just might not be true, but to you, in that moment, it feels sufficiently like it that you persist with the attitude and behaviours that somehow make it seem like it is absolute fact.

Your behaviours will change (in relation to what you are telling yourself is the 'truth'), you begin to project anxiety, panic, tension, fear, uncertainty, doubt. These emotional responses may be just what is needed.

I'm not referring here to real emergencies (such as fire or flood), but the potential, imagined kind.

Take action when that extreme moment shows up, precisely when you become aware of your physical or visceral response. Call a brief halt, step aside, go somewhere away from 'the action', grab a pen and paper if it helps. What are you actually carrying as your current truth? What is the unspoken phrase echoing in your head that describes your situation?

Write it down: describe, as best you can, your current predicament and experience.

I'm sure there is enough supportive evidence for you to put down your pen and carry on, but for the sake of this Impact Note, pause and deeply contemplate what else might be true? Could there be counter-evidence? How much of your experience is your own interpretation?

What 'truth' would you prefer, honestly? How would you prefer to work today?

Perhaps write down this aspirational truth as a new, improved descriptive sentence. Pause again, and contemplate what evidence exists right now, however scarce, that could underpin this new truth right now.

In following this approach you are actively jolting your fixed or default mode, shifting what you look for and notice. You are neutralizing your mood and attitude, ready for a more powerful, empowered, impactful upgrade.

If you act chaotically you will absolutely prove to yourself that chaos is all around you. If you wear a frown most days and grit your teeth, most events you encounter will be consistent with this mask. Change it, it might not be true.

ACTION:

CHANGING YOU, CHANGING THE WORLD

"YOU MUST BE THE CHANGE YOU WISH TO SEE IN THE WORLD."

Mahatma Gandhi

INSPIRED ACTION IS THE CREATOR, CATALYST AND CRYSTALLIZER OF IMPACT. HOW YOU AFFECT SITUATIONS, PEOPLE AND COMMUNITIES DIRECTLY INFLUENCES THE EFFECT YOU HAVE ON THE WORLD. YOUR DAY-TO-DAY CONDUCT CAN INITIATE AND MAINTAIN REAL-LIFE, EVERYDAY MOMENTUM. YOUR PERSONAL AND PROFESSIONAL QUALITIES WILL INSPIRE OTHERS TO ACT AND YOUR VISION AND LEADERSHIP IMPACT WILL EXTEND FURTHER THROUGH THE ACTIONS YOU INSPIRE THEM TO TAKE.

38. IT COULD BE YOU!

You could be the one – it only takes one person to be calm in the midst of chaos for calm to spread. It only takes one person to notice the discrepancy and correction begins. It takes one person to stand firm and the wave of change begins. It may not necessarily be noticeable, but all change, all 'sorting out', all inspirational new things ultimately begin with one person.

Don't just join the prevailing mood; where you feel, see or hear the need for change, for an intervention, where your quiet voice of intuition suggests something new is needed or perhaps something needs to stop, shake it up.

It could be you.

How do you know if it is?

It will be that issue, that discomfort, that irritation, that "why doesn't someone do something about that" feeling; something to which you have become accustomed to waiting for, or a situation you have long wished was different.

It could be you that your team, friends, colleagues, customers, are waiting for. It has become too easy, too comfortable, to accept situations (and grumble about them), you could be the change.

I invite you to switch on your awareness and increase your impact, so that when a situation arises in future (it could even be today) when you wish things were different in some way, I challenge you to be the one, be the change.

The change you begin will not necessarily be dramatic or ground-breaking, it may initially be subtle, often undetected, like the person who chooses calm in the midst of panic. Other examples:

- Decline meetings in an endless back-to-back conference culture, and relish the extra time you'll have.

- Choose a happy mode when the common attitude is grimacing, intense or miserable.

- Adopt a slow and measured pace in your movement and communication in chaotic, frantic environments.

- When everyone around you is putting down the situation or a particular person, state your true feelings rather than siding with them.

See Further Reading on page 161 for the link to a three-minute talk by musician, writer and entrepreneur (and former circus clown)

Derek Sivers at TED in 2010, about how to start a movement, the role of leadership and the crucial role of the first mover.

Practise this skill, at first in lower-risk situations. It is fundamental to all leadership, to your potentially profound leadership impact.

Once a month, take yourself away from your regular work environment and consider the areas in your world that irritate you, slow you down, or cause error or pain. Choose one and start your movement of change.

It only takes one person to bring about change; that person could be you. There is a role to be played in making improvements, it could be your role. The world may be waiting for you to make a start.

It only takes one person to make it start; it could be you. There is a role to be played, it could be you. The world is waiting.

39. SINGLE-MINDEDNESS MADE SIMPLE

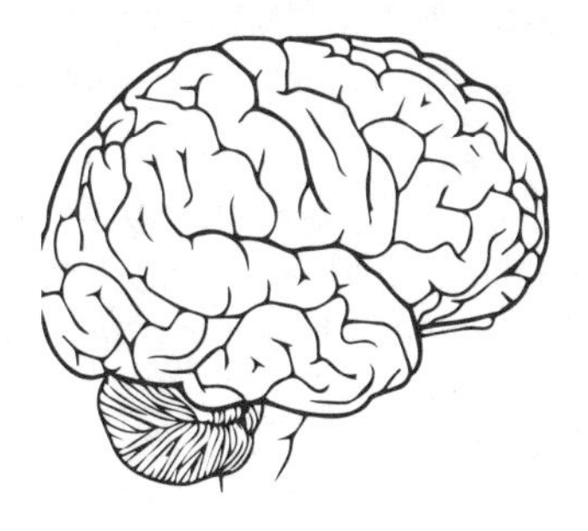

The value and benefit of being single-minded is often extolled. Many leaders with impact display single-mindedness in their ability to focus. More gets done if you are single-minded, with greater accuracy and accelerated personal progress; without this quality you get lost, distracted, overwhelmed and caught in the mire of details. Being single-minded is not just territory for the gurus, and the greatest of leaders, it is for you too.

Much has been written, taught, preached and advised about the value and power of becoming singled-minded. You consider highly those who can access a Zen-like state and have the ability to focus on one item, one task or even one thought. Its power leads these people to deep insights, inspired action, clarity, certainty and purposeful decision. But is this just the domain of those sitting cross-legged in serene silence, or is it attainable for you and me?

This Impact Note seeks to inspire you to create a clearer, simpler, more accessible pathway to your latent single-minded power.

It is a given that you can be single-minded. It's in your raw potential, you have unlearned the skill as the world has bombarded you with options, choices, challenges, decisions, (artificial and real) urgencies. In the past, you may have relied on a particular set of circumstances to create the 'ideal' moment for single-mindedness. If you were presented with an extreme situation, where extreme could be the urgency (and importance), the nature or scale of the threat (to you or others), may have enabled you to access your innate single-minded capability. The situation will have created the context in which your single-minded skills are revealed, naturally.

So why is this indisputable skill so difficult to access at all other times?

Well, you have immense gifts of thought and an abundance of choice about what you think about. Your life today is incredibly full, the volume of conversations, visual, audible and emotional stimuli are plentiful. The world seems to have become incredibly complex, hindering any chance of single-mindedness, without booking an afternoon off and going on a trip to a remote hill (and don't dismiss that as an option, by the way!).

It takes conscious, deliberate intention to rediscover your power of laser-like focus.

1. Review my Simple Notes 'Urgentia', '3-4-3' and 'Simple Meditation for the Busy Leader' at the simontyler.com blog or find a copy of *The 'Keep It Simple' Book.*

2. Define your ability and true stamina for an honest, realistic, concerted focus time (for most people it is around 20 minutes).

3. Carve out a three-hour period in your upcoming week's schedule and chop it into several SMS (single-minded sessions). This equates to nine sessions if your focus time is 20 minutes.

4. Decide on the topics that will become your single focus for the session.

5. Clear all distractions, move away, work somewhere protected from them, gather all the resources you will need.

6. As new thoughts come in and take your focus away, notice them and let them go.

For the first few sessions cut yourself some slack and alternate a 20 minute SMS with normal activity for next 20 minutes, where you get on with anything and everything.

You never know, this may become your new way of working. Good luck.

Your alternative is not to bother and carry on multi-tasking, moving from feeling overwhelmed to disappointed and back again, hoping something else or someone else will change it for you, or, that another emergency situation sparks your SMS.

Go on, you can (if you think you can).

The request to "mind the gap" is often made during announcements in London's underground stations due to the wide gap between platform and train; my regular travel through the city means the phrase has constantly 'spoken to me' and inspired me to explore its multiple meanings. This, perhaps my favourite Impact Note, unravels and puts to use this metaphor.

The busier you are, the more distracted you will become, the less time seems to be left for you to be creative, or to be in any way proactive and deliberate about the impact you could have. Yet, hidden in your everyday mayhem are opportunities for the creative subconscious to speak up. It is just a simple mindful step away.

My simplest observation about the business world today is that the pace is picking up, confidence in self, team, company and marketplaces is tentatively building after a long period of inward-looking caution. People have been 'full' and scrambling around for a while. They are still scrambling, but more often working on future-focused activity rather than rationalizing the past, or critically dissecting the present.

Increasingly, my clients and their teams talk of less time to think, never finding a moment to be personally strategic, in their roles, in their careers. And as a result they feel a mix of exhilaration (from the positivity of the new work) and nagging frustration (that things still aren't what they want them to be).

In such circumstances I also observe low levels of original thought, creative thinking, idea exploration and expansion, without having to set-up a formal, structured time to be specific! And the same addiction to urgency (read Simple Note 'Urgentia' in *The 'Keep It Simple' Book* to work directly on this unhelpful habit).

Until you are inspired and ready to be deliberate and unambiguously purposeful with your time, your choices will simply not access the awesome power of your own thinking and potential.

Your gift is the gap. In fact, not one, but noticing and grasping the plethora of, until now, unnoticed gaps between everything you do. You are already unconsciously using these gifts, I encourage you to become more aware of the gaps, to grasp them, shift your attitude to them, honour them and allow gaps to become mind-expanding super-simple spaces.

I'm referring to the time between meetings, the moment you lean back from your laptop, close your eyes and breathe, the extra minute standing in line for your morning coffee (formerly known as an irritation), shower time (or bathtime for the opulent-wash indulgers), waiting on the platform for the delayed 07:12, pausing as latecomers arrive and settle before your meeting. Your gaps could be as short as seconds or extend to several minutes. More than that, and the gap becomes a more obvious work-session for which you will probably have other plans, and habitual ways of using.

Your current gap-response will be to access an unhelpful emotion; irritation, frustration, anxiety, annoyance, which change your mood to a less-than-helpful state. You may habitually fill those tiny gaps with a glance at your mobile, download emails, re-read or send a text, play a game, visit a sport website. Yet, quietly in the background, your higher self (brain, mind, soul, spirit... choose what works for you) is delighted with the gap and turns up the volume on latent ideas, inspiration, half-formed thoughts, spots clues, initiates an inkling. You may be drowning out these gentle background intuitive sounds, but they're still there, striking a gentle tone.

Tune in, be mindful, and grasp the gap. Notice the gap when it arrives, cherish it, honour it, sit still, breathe deeply, walk casually and simply let it be... a glorious gap. And by the way, there is undeniable evidence of gaps being the place in which new ideas, new businesses, products and services spawn. How many times have you had new thoughts, ideas, and insightful questions after just a few moments' pause?

You will be pleasantly surprised, or perhaps even shocked, at what you can come up with when your gaps are allowed, simply, to be. Go on, 'mind the gap!'

41. 10 SIGNS OF COMPLEXITY OVERLOAD

Great leaders thrive on a clear vision, a distinct direction which is visible for others to follow. Your role as a leader is to provide that vision, particularly in uncertain times and when circumstances become complex and confused. As sure as the sun rises each day, situations, projects, programmes, people grow complicated. This looming complexity tests the strength of your vision and your ability to work through it.

Through my coaching and mentoring relationships, I have observed how everyday pressures affect working practices, diminishing the effect of this essential leadership skill. In effect, the advance of complexity is exacerbated by the leaders themselves and the opportunity for positive change is missed.

It is your job to simplify. In fact, the potency of your leadership impact depends upon it.

And it starts with you, your methods for handling complexity.

Complexity is a curious thing. It tends to creep up on you quietly until, almost without noticing, you have become consumed by it and in it, and from there the route out requires some pretty serious work. The longer you leave it until you recognize and accept that you are 'in complexity', the tougher it is to shift. Catch it early, and you can turn, inspirationally, towards simplicity where others flounder.

I have observed 10 commonly recurring signs that show complexity has reached the point of overload.

This Impact Note has two objectives. The first is obviously to help and inspire you in some way, to address your complexities. The second is to clarify the signs, by inviting you to examine the list below, confirm those that apply to you and add to the list, from your experience of managing your own complexities.

My coaching experience has confirmed that personal development action is absolutely necessary if you are experiencing one or more of the following signs of complexity overload:

1. Your levels of stress and anxiety are increasing (or have obvious peaks).

2. Your 'fuse' seems shorter (before your react inappropriately).

3. Your ability to motivate yourself is more difficult and burns for less than a few hours at a time.

4. Your ability to motivate others takes more effort than you seem to have available.

5. Your work environments are increasingly disorganized.

6. The number of tabs/files/emails open on your computer screen at any one time is more than three.

7. Everything you are working on, everything in your in-tray/in-box, everything you are focusing on, seems urgent.

8. Your ability to concentrate fully on a task is down to 10 minutes or less at a time (before distractions easily lure away your attention).

9. You become entangled in minutiae which, on reflection later, was largely irrelevant.

10. You hesitate and delay decisions (and the deferred decision list is accumulating).

There are many other signs of complexity overload but my research suggests that these 10 are the most frequent.

- How many of the signs of overload are you displaying?

- How many of the signs do you notice in friends and colleagues around you?

Ignoring them and 'coping with them', which in reality means accepting them, can only ever be a short-term strategy.

There will be an Impact Note in this book that will help you and your colleagues so go ahead and inspire the change. The antidotes to each of these signs of complexity are fairly obvious, but only through noticing them actively and taking intentional corrective action will you make the change.

Signs one to four are asking for relaxation, reflection, downtime and space; taking a moment to reconnect what you are doing with your purpose, goal and vision. At the busiest times (which may have led to the signs showing up) there are no better investments for your time than to take the counter-complex-action, but your inner voices may demand you stay 'on-task' (and make the signs even more obvious).

Signs five to seven are asking for a conscious and deliberate de-cluttering. Again, this investment of time will pay dividends, and quickly. Your mind is attempting to process everything on your desk and on-screen, at the same time. Your personal RAM is being used up. You may well have be suffering from Urgentia (see my Simple Note 'Urgentia' in *The 'Keep It Simple' Book*), where everything seems urgent and you have lost the ability to make a distinction between the important and unimportant.

Signs 8 to 10 are calling on the leader inside; step away, get some distance on the situation, take counsel, decide (see Impact Note 32 'Decision Glue' on page 101), and re-engage.

Turn on your self-awareness, notice your state and mood, and take the counter-complex-action.

42. WILL IT MAKE THE BOAT GO FASTER?

As the volume of work increases, and the mix of stakeholders demands a wider range of activities, you can lose sight of what is important, and what is taking you towards your goals. This Impact Note uses an Olympic medal-winning principle to regain focus.

Great Britain rowing gold medalist Ben Hunt-Davis talks about his team's transformation from consistent middle-ranking performers to 2000 Sydney Olympics Gold medal winners.

The rowing eight faced a number of challenges, and many critical aspects of its performance were almost good enough, but not quite. The crew members didn't all get on, often wasting time arguing, seeking to prove they were more right than their team-mates in any particular debate. Individualism, while an immensely powerful driver, was more divisive than decisive.

The focus point on which their dramatic transformation took place was the simple question, "will it make the boat go faster?", which ultimately became the title of Ben's book (see Further Reading on page 161).

This question instantly took discussion to the new bottom-line of anything and everything that was part of their preparation for the Olympics. It cut through debates, sharpened decisions and took the potentially fractious crew to agreement and acceptance. This included, in some cases, reducing training sessions, changing diets and altering the structure of meetings and discussions.

The translation and application to business situations was obvious and undeniable.

The simple question most easily applies in sport, and specifically the pursuit of a single goal (for example Olympic gold). But, of course, almost every business situation has multiple goals, multiple measures and a mixture of stakeholders, not a single and obvious first place.

However, this should not become a reason to avoid levelling the question.

I encourage you to consider your personal journey and that of your team, division or company, and pose the simple question "will it make the boat go faster?"

What might the three versions of 'faster' be for you? Is there a definitive metric? When it comes down to it, what is most important? What are you (or your team) really setting out to achieve?

Proving how right you are, winning petty battles, completing habitual tasks, mindless meetings, extended working days, suddenly stand out as having little or no impact on your metaphorical boat speed.

Noticing your work patterns, your mental and physical fatigue levels, the impact you have on others and the impact they have on you will reap you much leadership impact reward.

Take your leadership goals and intent (having articulated it of course), in terms of who you are, what you stand for and where you are taking your team and company. Look at the week or month ahead. Will the activities and events in your schedule, the meetings, the projects, the stakeholder relationships actually make you leadership boat go faster?

Apply this to your career goal, the role or leadership situation to which you aspire, the impact you wish to have in your marketplace or on the world.

Review what you were up to over the previous seven days, who you met, what you created, the actions you chose (and those you chose not to take or to delay). Have they made your career and impact boat go faster? You decide, it's not going to row itself.

43. ACORN REPAIR STRATEGIES

Throughout your career, for both business and personal reasons, you invest a significant quantity of your time in activities and strategies to repair situational errors. Errors and breaks in processes, patterns, people and performance. Sometimes, though, a recurrent breakage is a clue that something new is attempting to emerge, rather than a fault needing fixing. The inspirational, impactful leader is one who can identify this as growth and work with it to nurture it to success.

For several years, unquestionably, the global business climate has been challenging. Everything seems to have changed or is in some form of breakdown and transition. Systems, processes, establishments, people, teams, expectations, work patterns that were once certain and predictable, are no longer reliable or even there at all.

I have worked and coached many in the banking and financial services sector, one which has faced more of this uncertainty than others. When the waves of change hit, I observed many reactions, responses, coping strategies, defence mechanisms and immense personal effort put into holding on or on restoring some semblance of certainty (temperament and behavioural studies confirm that we have a need for an amount of certainty and uncertainty, which for most of us are, at times, out of balance).

When working through some material by Law of Emergence guru Derek Rydall (see Further Reading on page 161), I picked up the acorn metaphor and was struck by how it captures what I have noticed over these turbulent years.

Acorns fall and split open and, for a while, lie dormant in a poor state of repair. In business, processes and systems (and people) fall and break too. Building an Acorn Repair Team may, for a while, return your stock of acorns to a beautiful state but the inevitable will occur. What is meant to emerge from those oak seeds will emerge, it is virtually an unstoppable natural force. Our 'repair work' may in fact delay, restrict, stunt or inhibit the full emergence of what is possible.

My intention with this Impact Note is to heighten your awareness of possible Acorn Repair Strategies in which you are inadvertently investing, within your business, your team or your own development. Could you, at least for a while, accept the disrepair and allow conversations to start from there (practising acceptance)?

Of course, damage must be repaired (whatever that might mean for you), so do that. Ongoing damage may, however, be a sign that something else is trying to emerge.

Good luck, keep it simple, and accept your acorns for what they are.

44. ONE STEP BEYOND

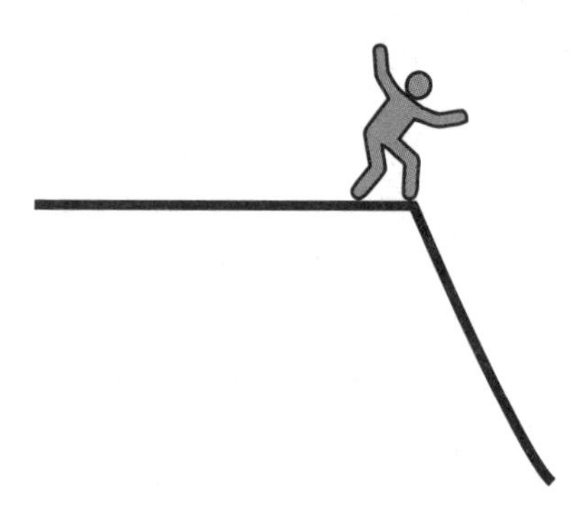

Are you stuck in a situation that needs to shift but the 'what' and the 'how' elude you? Often you become caught in the gripping need to follow a 'think, think, think' strategy to make change. This Impact Note presents a way forward.

I have met, and continue to meet, many senior professionals who are wrestling with their current situation in some way. It could be their job role, their company's current cultural direction or atmosphere, relationships, health, or simply the nagging sense that they should be doing something else.

This type of growing unease is centred on things (people, circumstances, patterns) not being how you want them to be, something has changed and you don't like it, or it needs changing, or you've been stuck in it for too long.

Despite the volume of thinking you may have pointed at it, or even the multiple corrective-change initiatives you have put in place, nothing has changed. All the thinking has done is to remind you of what isn't right each time you return to it, further compounding the frustration, creating a sensation of commercial impotence, of being trapped. This feeling could perhaps have spread and led to you becoming uncertain or even scared to take action in many other areas of your life as well.

When this trapped feeling manifests itself and clarity of action is absent, deeper work is needed rather than 'think, think, think' internal investigation.

The point of this Impact Note may seem counter-intuitive and initially meet with your internal logical resistance but if you can find the strength to follow it, you will rapidly experience a shift.

The fastest way to become a magnet to new ideas and inspire new creative thinking is to deal with what you have in front of you right now, with the resources you have available at this moment in time.

That's it, with the following enhancement steps:

- If you are doing it (whatever 'it' is), do it well. So, if you are writing, write a lot; if you're leading a meeting, hone your performance, presence and concentration.

- Observe what others do and how they behave when involved in similar tasks, note best practice and experiment with learned styles or techniques.

- Try new things, do something different (be radically creative; for example, change the order, multiply the units by 10, change location).

- Take tiny improvement steps, constantly (this counteracts the feeling of becoming stuck or the desire to give up).

The greatest opportunity you have for achieving positive change is getting stuck into the 'now' stuff around you immediately, rather than superficially (idling, waiting for the next step to be presented to you by someone or something else). Only then will it become obvious to you what to do next and, soon after, the resources you need will come to hand. It will become clear.

On your way, fear, uncertainty and doubt may still rear up ahead of you. Face the fears as they arise, no sooner. Notice how you have been facing and attempting to tackle fears that do not yet exist (futile?).

And, just sometimes, while you are reconnecting with what is in front of you, you will see it anew, as if for the first time (apologies to poet T. S. Eliot for misusing that line).

45. THE MIDDLE WAY

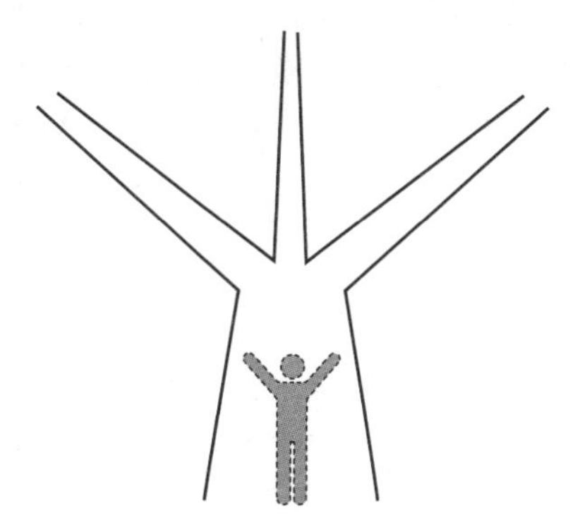

Choosing the middle way is a no-brainer: charting a course through life's extremes is both sensible and necessary. True leadership is not about making rash, flashy decisions. Finding the middle way is the most likely, most certain way through any tough situation, and yet it is the route least chosen.

If you have read any Buddhist work or teachings you will have come across the expression "the middle way". This is the simple life journey guidance of finding a path between the extremes of austerities and sensual indulgence.

I am inspired and profoundly aligned with this thinking. The middle way is very simple. Keep it simple and you will find the balance for which you have been yearning. Extremes are fear-based and destructive to you and those around you, often are imagined, not real and provoke emotional reactions in our behaviour that perpetuate the erratic progress.

The current commercial world today is turbulent, the demand for change and immediate corrective action is all too frequent. As a leader, you are called to change your path often. If you bend to these demands every time, the route along which you are leading others becomes tortuous, seemingly random and uncomfortable.

Choosing the middle way could be the context in which your leadership impact is communicated more effectively.

Situations such as disappointing sales results, lower-than-expected income levels, reductions in performance, loss of connection and collaboration across teams, loss of morale and motivation, pointlessness, lack of purpose, feeling overwhelmed, a sense of defeat, self-doubt. You and your stakeholders begin to crave the opposite, the extreme opposite and now!

Under the misleading banner of radical creativity, I have noticed clients and client companies, faced with such situations, adopting extreme counter-strategies to steer out of trouble. The actions taken, while occasionally delivering a short-term win, only perpetuate and accelerate the swing of the pendulum. When you spend significant amounts of time trying to maintain an extreme, nothing moves forward. It appears that you have momentum but in reality you are carving a deep rut, in which you will soon become stuck. You become stuck there, in your self-made trench, working too hard or too little, increasing fatigue levels and allowing self-doubt to return.

The next time you face an extreme, notice and feel the emotional response (such as when someone cuts you up in traffic). Just monitor it, from the perspective of the observer; your relationship to the 'extreme' instantly changes, allowing you to make positive, impactful choice of the middle way.

Here are some thoughts to help you find your middle way:

1. Immediately ask yourself to define the two extreme responses that you could choose – this instantly jolts your brain into realizing there must be a middle response too.

2. Take a pause, especially if you are not naturally a reflective type.

3. Run a sweep of your resources (people, time, funds, equipment, and space) assessing which are in full use and which are not – this can often inspire a creative new approach using what is here already, but differently.

4. Where are you feeling pressure (physical and mental)?, what steps could you take to relieve that (stand up, stretch, breathe, release, let go, pass on, delegate)?

And, by the way, it's ok that your pendulum swings. In fact, it has to at first, to show where the middle might lie. As soon as you stop the swinging you will find yourself filled with more energy (energy that was, until now, wasted on the extremes).

It takes a deep dive into the reserves of your leadership strength to find and pursue a middle way. All around you others will be calling, imploring that you take massive (hasty) counter-action. A middle way response may not deliver remarkable, immediate change. Sceptics and cynics will challenge your strategic decisions.

And this, in and of itself, is also indicative of an environment or company or team that is habitually caught in the extremes.

This is a moment for the impact of you, your leadership moment. Lead, have impact, follow your middle way.

46. SIMPLIFY, NOW?

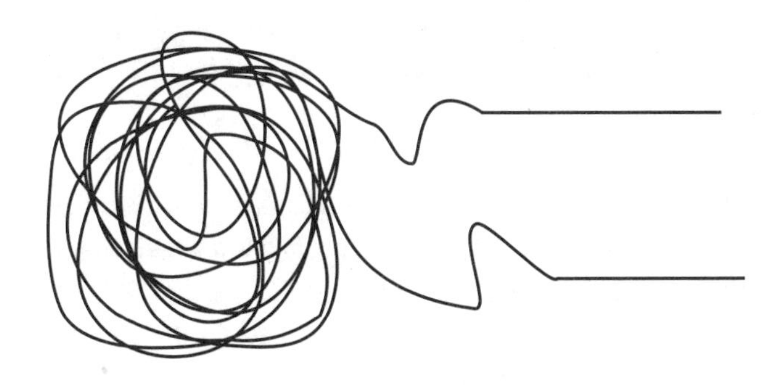

Could you possibly be playing a part in the complexity of your current circumstance? Reality often overwhelms you and dictates the way you operate, the reactions and responses you have. Hidden in there is your incredible ability to cause it to be different, simpler even. An easier everyday experience is possible, it's up to you.

Business is tough. Finding and securing new clients or sales or agreements is more difficult today than previously. There is more to consider, more to absorb, wider implications for everything in which you are involved. You may even not allow yourself to experience any degree of happiness unless your situation changes. Have you become hooked on making things tougher than they really are or need to be?

But life is complicated.

Your current reality is packed full of evidence that this is the case. And to think and act differently is naive and delusional, isn't it?

The thing with reality, is, quite obviously, that it is real, and it is right now. But here is my challenge with this Impact Note. Reality is not, in fact, now.

Reality is the accumulated stuff that occurred or existed right up until the moment before this one, but not in this moment. From here you can decide what your reaction is to that 'reality' and, indeed, what your next reality could be. Yes, you can do this despite the seemingly unstoppable force of your 'current' circumstance.

A common habit I have noticed in clients and client companies is that they harbour the learned and ingrained expectation that things are difficult; anything easier than difficult must be wrong, not thorough enough or lucky.

This simply perpetuates complexity.

There is one simple step for you to take to enable things to become easier than they are for you now:

Expect them to be easier.

The resistance you experience to this challenge instantly highlights the barriers currently in place preventing you from allowing it to become true (and, by the way, there is immense personal development value in identifying them, challenging them and releasing them).

Your everyday experience could be easier than you are currently urging it to be.

Experiment with the following exercise.

Take a moment...

... and list the situations, projects, people, environments that appear to be complicated. You may even experience a physical sensation as you think about them, a tightening of your chest, neck or shoulders.

Now consider...

... how you would relate or engage with the situation if it were simpler. When pared back, what is the raw, simple truth about, your connection to it, your hopes and expectations for it? What can be taken out of the situation?

Begin again from there, act as if it were simpler, expect it to be so.

Go on, defy your current reality.

47. YOUR DIGITAL MINDSET

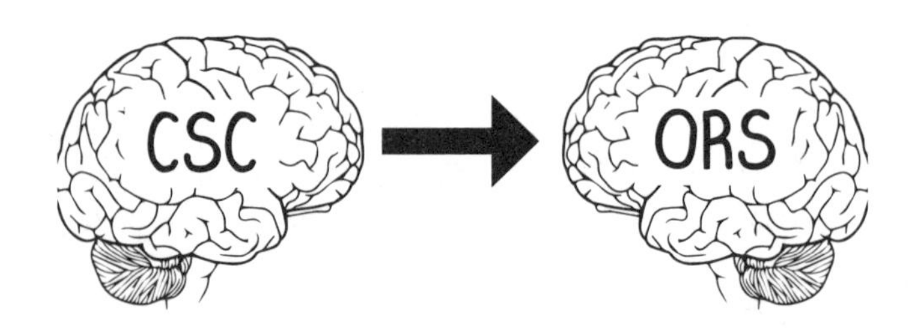

The volume, proliferation and inundation of information today may cause you discomfort, and your way of handling it is the focus of this Impact Note. How you engage with it all, lead others through it and make it work for you, defines your impact potential.

Social networks (Facebook, LinkedIn, Twitter, Google+ and so on) are challenging what, and how, you connect and share anything.

How you handle the digital world and its flow of information, your sources and your networks, may define your success (in using them to your advantage), easing stress levels, increasing personal efficiency, growth and igniting positive personal change.

Thomas Power, the founder and chairman of Ecademy coined two acronyms that capture the journey each of us is challenged to make in this information and networking transition journey. He spoke brilliantly on this topic a few years ago at a TEDxNewStreet conference (an independently-organized TED event and detailed in Further Reading on page 161).

Corporations, and the tardiness in many of us, he describes as being CSC:

- Closed – to new ideas, methods, ways, channels, people.
- Selective – about the people and places with whom you connect, work and from whom you source.
- Controlling – of the people in our circle, of their activity, methods and ways of working.

Being CSC is not wrong, or bad. It quite probably has been a valuable, often principled, protective way to be, in the information-prolific world of the past. However, staying closed, selective and controlling is now requiring more effort and your decisions and standards are challenged daily. It may even feel like you're fighting a losing battle. The more you entrench, the more difficult it has, or will, become.

Today demands that you question your operating methods and methods of connection to the flow of information. Often, children have a completely different way of living in the digital world and sitting in the flow and more of Thomas Power's assertions are found to be present in their use of media.

My own children are, to use Power's second and antithesis acronym, ORS:

- Open – to all channels, willing to experiment and explore, prepared to do things wrong first.

- Random - resisting the need to force structure and order, resisting judging anything (at least initially).

- Supportive - of anyone in their new networks, prepared to be part of the process of change and experimentation, happy to be part of almost any network or collective (at least initially).

Your transition from CSC to ORS will take time and will not necessarily be easy, but it is a journey that will bring rewards, in new information, less anxiety and a preparedness for whatever happens next in the information-flowing world.

Obviously, this could be a coaching-supported journey (find a coach), and certainly a path that is easier to travel with colleagues than alone.

The same transition will apply to your team and your company. The sooner it is made, the faster the benefits will be noticed.

48. SIMPLIFYING MEETING MADNESS

Unless you work on your own, for yourself, or in some chosen or enforced isolation, your weekly schedule will likely be peppered with meetings: meetings about your projects, team members' projects, corporate information-sharing, programme updates and on and on.

The culture in your organization has possibly led to the habit of multiple invitations and equally habitual acceptance and attendance. What was once a conversation, then a meeting, has become a forum or even a committee.

The time left to be creative, space to think, opportunities to build relationships, to extend your leadership impact, has reduced down to a few moments a day. And, so often, these chances are in the margins at the beginning or end of the day or even squeezed into travel time, or during (once sacrosanct) personal time... evenings and weekends.

If you truly desire positive change, to create something new for you, your team or your company, then the time must surely have come for you to check your meeting habits.

I have often found inspiration in the thinking and working practices of the late co-founder and CEO of Apple Inc Steve Jobs and this Impact Note about meetings is dedicated to him.

Jobs instilled, within Apple, the principle of meetings populated by the lowest possible number of participants. Unless someone was critical to the decision or had something crucial to add, they were asked, bluntly, to leave the meeting.

Start with small groups of smart people, every time the number increases, unnecessary complexity increases with it.

To access the best of simplicity, and have most potent impact, not least speed, I provocatively suggest that the more critical a project in which you are involved, the fewer smart people you co-opt in. This is the opposite of most corporate behaviour. Common practice is where the fear of exclusion, fear of making decisions without every single corner involved, consulted and given voice, means delay, deferral and even avoidance.

Here is a bonus meeting culture changer: never allow a meeting to run beyond 30 minutes.

Anything longer than this changes the emphasis, behaviour and approach. Meetings become working parties, discussion rooms, and opinion airings. Impact reduces with every minute after half-an-hour.

Go on, challenge your meeting behaviour, keep it simple and boost your impact.

49. NUCLEAR TIME MANAGEMENT

Like most of my clients you, during your career, have probably continued to seek out methods of enhancing your productivity, sharpening your focus and increasing your leadership impact. The pressures on you as a leader today make it even tougher to get the most out of yourself and your teams. The way in which we now live, work, think and operate calls for an alternative set of techniques to alter our relationship with time in a positive manner.

During my corporate career I attended many 'time management' programmes and initiatives and, on the way, picked up an array of techniques and attitudes that, for a while, sharpened my focus, enhanced my productivity and made me organized.

In the late 1990s, I put together a number of workshops and learning modules incorporating the best of those previously-learned time skills, together with what I had observed in the best time-use practitioners.

Since then, my focus has been on people like you, and the challenges you face, particularly in terms of time-choices, in today's environment. In previous years, the popular and oft-proffered techniques did not have to contend with today's scores of emails, meetings, continuous social connections, messaging and the demand for all leaders to be able to multi-task, at pace, day-after-day.

How you use your time, the choices you make, absolutely and directly affect your impact.

It is no longer possible to hold, rigidly, to a fixed timetable, nor to be certain of what is going to show up each day. The ability to park new requests and challenges until you are ready to evaluate them is for managers of the past.

Consider the following list of my top 10 nuclear time management tips and experiment and implement those that resonate for you.

- **Gap excellence** – notice, capture and cherish all your gaps (see Impact Note 40 'Mind the Gap' page 126).

- **Standing-room only** – change some of your meetings (particularly those via teleconferencing) to have participants standing. This physical change in their stance can alter mood and mode, inputs tend to be shorter, eye contact better, listening skills improve, connection is stronger, fewer notes are taken, there is a truer commitment to outcomes.

- **New start time** – switch the start time of meetings and appointments to any time other than on the engrained and habitual hour or half-hour.

- **New running time –** set the meeting length to anything other than 30 or 60 minutes (or multiples thereof). Combining tip three and tip four works well, for example, meeting at 10.20 for 25 minutes, creates a heightened awareness of the actual time in the minds of participants, who tend to honour the new timing, and meeting behaviour shifts accordingly.

- **Stop at the how –** this is one of my favourites, having observed rooms full of high-powered, highly-paid executives getting stuck into lists and methods and approaches of 'how' to make a change. You and your team are naturally awesome at 'how to-ing' anything, with best ideas and results taking place after and away from meetings, that's what your creative sub-conscious loves to get on with, so leave it to its devices. Stop meetings when 'how' conversations begin and send that challenge out of the room.

- **My days –** mark out a day or a part-day regularly (you decide what regularly is, weekly, fortnightly, monthly, for example) and only work on your strategic or future-focused projects; no emails, no texts, no phone, no meetings, nothing, just your stuff. You'll need a heap of strength to stay focused on this tip, so set it up carefully, sleep well the night before, maintain your fluids and eat healthily.

- **Bio basics –** be honest, you are better at certain times of the day than others and at certain times of the months than others. You are affected positively by events and people and, without doubt, you are affected negatively by certain events and people too. Bio Basics is tuning into these cycles and building your days and weeks accordingly. Stop depleting your resources trying to be a version of yourself that isn't quite available. When you are fizzing and feeling great it would be inefficient and personally sub-optimal to fill your time with meetings; instead, have more one-to-ones, meet people, strategize, and create spaces to think bigger. Make a list of your main three modes (for example, 'fizzing', 'settled' and 'flat'), then list the typical events in which you are involved (meetings with colleagues, one-to-one appointments, meeting customers, being creative, writing, deep admin) and decide which mode is best matched to which event. Then you can honestly know what to expect (from yourself) and where you can really stretch yourself (and perhaps even source a 'do not disturb' sign for those top-rated creative times).

- **Listen twice, cut once** – this is a counter-technique to what I notice as commonplace in corporate situations. What does busyness do to you? How do you behave during extremely busy times, days, weeks? Often, listening skills are impaired (yours and probably the skills of many members of your team), the likelihood of error increases markedly, every time. The pressure to remember minutiae, sometimes critical pieces of information, is too great. Listen twice, cut once is a radical measure that protects everyone's time and reduces errors. Hold a second meeting (several hours or a couple of days later) to discuss/present exactly the same information. A second pass catches errors early.

- **Interrupt me now** – as you lead more and more people, as your impact broadens, more of them will want a piece of you, your comment, your approval, your insight, your advice. Initially this feels great, soon it becomes annoying, and shortly after that you notice the effect these interruptions have on your productivity. Your impact is blunted. Be clear and fair with those you lead, set and communicate 'interrupt me now' times. This means times when you are doing low-risk, administrative tasks not requiring your deepest thoughts, allowing you to become brilliant at brief snatched conversations, always being 'fully present' with those in front of you.

- **Write it down** – for a month, keep a journal and track your activity, your ideas, your observations and your mood. Go to your journal as often as you can during the day. This technique works in a number of ways. First, it provides you with some data about your peak and pit times. Second, it gets you used to journaling, which is a mindful technique used in some form by most of the world's inspirational leaders. Third, it captures those floating thoughts and part-formed ideas and conversations that may get lost in the smog of a busy week.

How you behaved, in relationship to time in the past, has got you where you are now, but is unlikely to get you to where you want to go. Upgrade now.

50. LEAN INTO

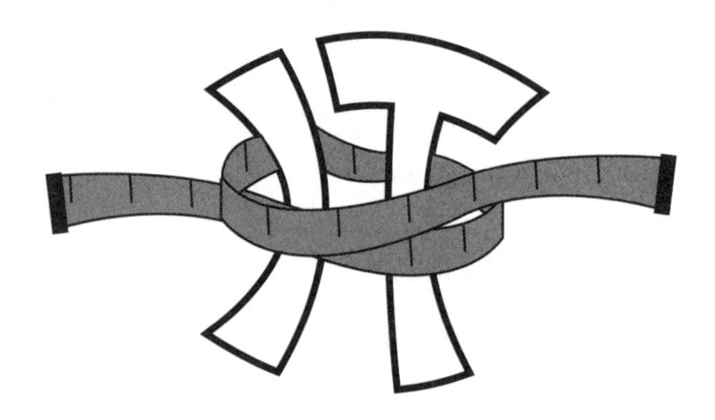

Lean leadership has impact.

Lean infers both your inclination, or angle of approach and also thin, efficient, no wastage or superfluous fat. Both definitions have an application in leadership.

'Lean' became an accepted concept in business some decades ago, used to describe the improvement of process flow and the elimination of waste (products and time), and was developed by the Toyota Motor Corporation. Lean is basically about getting the right things to the right place, at the right time, in the right quantities, while minimizing waste and being flexible and open to change and further development.

Could this, in some way, describe your leadership style?

Lean applies to your business – cutting out the unnecessary and low value-adding activities.

Lean applies to your thinking – cutting out thoughts that make you feel bad in any way.

I have worked with a few leaders and managers who have been formally trained and accredited in this philosophy (and six sigma, for example). Having become utterly immersed in the concepts, they habitually evaluate how they and their teams are operating and take deliberate steps to become leaner, often.

Each time I have introduced 'lean' into a coaching conversation with an individual or a team, something positive has happened. It is a simple question and framework for focusing and simplifying.

This Impact Note seeks to bring your attention equally to the other definition of lean.

The angle of your approach.

I can hear Maggie, my personal trainer, urging me again and again to 'lean into it'. And, in one of my sessions with her, I made the obvious connection. More of your potential, your strength, your reserves of energy and power are accessed when you shift your inclination (and therein sits another multi-applicable definition).

I now urge you to lean into whatever you are working on, physically, mentally. It's the fastest way to make progress and the fastest way for new opportunities to find a way to show up and for you to become a magnet for new ideas.

Here are four simple 'lean into it' ideas:

- Actually think of your stance – when you are at the gym, when you are presenting, when you are sitting at the meeting table or even your desk – shift your angle of approach.

- Pick up the pace, increase the volume and frequency – for a short period of time, an hour, a day, a week.

- Go too far – only through testing and stretching accepted boundaries can you find out the extent of what is possible. Test your and your team's resilience and stamina. (Cautionary note: be safe when it comes to going too far, build in buffers, support, checks and balances.)

- Try something new – your approach to meetings, methods, techniques, explore previously ignored wacky ideas.

If you want something (a change, a role, a shift of some kind), stop waiting or engaging passively in the task, instead lean into it.

FURTHER READING AND INFORMATION

On your way through this book you will have noticed a number of resources that have inspired me, often specifically, to write that particular Impact Note.

Here they are, with other sources of inspiration that I did not directly mention.

BOOKS:

Dr Wayne W. Dyer, *I Can See Clearly Now*, 2014, Hay House, Inc.

Dr Wayne W. Dyer, *Change Your Thoughts, Change Your Life*, 2007, Hay House, Inc.

Dr Wayne W. Dyer, *Living the Wisdom of the Tao*, 2008, Hay House, Inc.

Stephen R Covey, *The Speed of Trust*, 2006, Simon & Schuster.

Daniel Goleman, *What Makes a Leader: Why Emotional Intelligence Matters,* 2014, More Than Sound.

Daniel Goleman, E*motional Intelligence: Why It Can Matter More Than I.Q.,* 1996, Bloomsbury Publishing PLC.

William James, *The Principles of Psychology, Vol. 1*, v1, 2013, Cosimo Classics.

Don Miguel-Ruiz *The Four Agreements,* 1997, Amber-Allen Publishing Inc.

Bill North, *True North*, 2007, John Wiley & Sons.

Gareth Jones and Rob Goffee, *Why Should Anyone Be Led By You?* 2006, Harvard Business Review Press.

Ben Hunt Davies, *Will It Make the Boat Go Faster*, 2011, Matador.

Eleanor, H. Porter, *Pollyana,* 2011, CreateSpace Independent Publishing Platform.

FILMS:

Dr Wayne W. Dyer, *"The Shift"*, 2009, Hay House, Inc.

The Pursuit of Happyness, 2007, Sony Pictures

VIDEOS:

Derek Sivers at TED in 2010, talks about how to start a movement, the role of leadership and the crucial role of the first mover.
www.ted.com/talks/derek_sivers_how_to_start_a_movement.html

Thomas Powers at TEDxNewStreet on the Future of Social Networks
https://www.youtube.com/watch?v=fVs6Zogzg4g

RESOURCES:

Aristotle, *Physics, Book IV*. Written 350, BCE. Translated by R. P. Hardie and R. K. Gaye, available at **http://classics.mit.edu/Aristotle/physics.4.iv.html**

Derek Rydall's Law of Emergence program **http://lawofemergence.com/activateyourpowerwithin/**

Scott Wintrip's blog **http://wintripconsultinggroup.com/blog/category/simply-effective/**

Saint Jérôme, Letter CV11, available at **http://biblehub.com/library/jerome/the_principal_works_of_st_jerome/letter_cvii_to_laeta.htm**

ABOUT THE AUTHOR

SIMON TYLER is an inspirational speaker and world class coach. His work with leaders, thinkers and creative entrepreneurs enables him to speak and write about his experience of coaching and mentoring successful people to lead and live with simplicity and impact.

His passionate belief and everyday philosophy is to create a space, clear away what is confusing, and then take action to clarify and simplify your interactions with the world. He has worked with hundreds of talented corporate clients to enhance their impact and professional practice in a way that transforms their approach to business and has led to undeniable measurable change in their personal, as well as commercial, lives.

Simon has worked one-to-one with over 1000 leaders and executives and have been hired by many leading and evolving global corporations, working with their teams and individually with leaders, and he is engaged privately by executives across the world.

His other title in the Concise Advice series, The 'Keep It Simple' Book, is the culmination of many years observing and noting the importance of simplicity and is a pragmatic guide, inviting readers to dispense with the personal and commercial pains of complecations and benefit from the rewards that the discipline of true simplicity brings. *The Impact Book* develops this thinking and provides clear, supportive and challenging steps to change the impact you have on the world.

It is his belief that if you take the time to reconsider the impact you have on others, you can truly inspire, and lead with purpose and meaning.

CONTACT THE AUTHOR FOR ADVICE, COACHING, MENTORING, FACILITATING AND SPEAKING

simon@simontyler.com
simontyler.com
thesimpleway.tv

in http://uk.linkedin.com/in/simontyler/
@simplysimont
simontyler_official
Simon Tyler – The Simplist

ALSO BY THE AUTHOR

- *The Simple Way* – published by Marshall Cavendish
- *The 'Keep It Simple' Book* – published by LID publishing
- *Simple Notes* – published on the web every two weeks, free subscription at **simontyler.com**
- Learning – the resource library of exercises, articles and deeper personal work at **simontyler.com.**